T0360628

ROUTLEDGE LIBRARY EDITIONS:
ENERGY

Volume 3

A DICTIONARY OF ENERGY

A DICTIONARY OF ENERGY

MARTIN COUNIHAN

Routledge
Taylor & Francis Group

LONDON AND NEW YORK

First published in 1981 by Routledge

This edition first published in 2019
by Routledge
2 Park Square, Milton Park, Abingdon, Oxon OX14 4RN

and by Routledge
52 Vanderbilt Avenue, New York, NY 10017

Routledge is an imprint of the Taylor & Francis Group, an informa business

© 1981 Martin Counihan

British Library Cataloguing in Publication Data
A catalogue record for this book is available from the British Library

ISBN: 978-0-367-21122-6 (Set)
ISBN: 978-0-429-26565-5 (Set) (ebk)
ISBN: 978-0-367-21111-0 (Volume 3) (hbk)
ISBN: 978-0-429-26555-6 (Volume 3) (ebk)

Publisher's Note
The publisher has gone to great lengths to ensure the quality of this reprint but points out that some imperfections in the original copies may be apparent.

Disclaimer
The publisher has made every effort to trace copyright holders and would welcome correspondence from those they have been unable to trace.

A Dictionary of **Energy**

Martin Counihan

ROUTLEDGE & KEGAN PAUL
London, Boston and Henley

To Elizabeth

First published in 1981
by Routledge & Kegan Paul Ltd
39 Store Street, London WC1E 7DD,
9 Park Street, Boston, Mass. 02108, USA, and
Broadway House, Newtown Road,
Henley-on-Thames, Oxon RG9 1EN
Set in IBM Press Roman by
Hope Services, Abingdon
and printed in Great Britain by
Redwood Burn Ltd
Trowbridge, Wiltshire

Library of Congress Cataloging in Publication Data

Counihan, Martin, 1945-

A dictionary of energy.
Bibliography: p.
1. Power (Mechanics)—Dictionaries. 2. Power
resources—Dictionaries. 3. Force and energy—
Dictionaries. I. Title.
TJ163.8.C68   621.042'03'21   81-8703

ISBN 0-7100-0847-3   AACR2

Contents

Figures

Contents

Tables

vi

Preface and acknowledgments

This dictionary is about energy: its nature, the forms it can take, its conversion and use, the fossil fuels and other sources, and the economics and politics of energy. As a desktop reference work, the book will be useful to staff in the relevant industries, governmental bodies, and research institutions, and educators will find it of great value as a source of material. Additionally, the book is aimed at the general reader and students of energy-related subjects, who I hope will find it stimulating, concise and inexpensive. It is expected that many will use this dictionary not merely for reference but also as a readable and systematic survey of the energy field, written factually and (to the author's occasional frustration) without lengthy discussion of the controversial issues. No axes are ground.

Energy is a fuzzy-edged subject in which one comes across specialised terms from all the engineering disciplines, the sciences, economics, and more besides; so an effort has had to be made to prevent this book from mushrooming into a dictionary of general science and engineering. Another problem has been that there are many words and phrases common in the energy context but having standard English meanings adequately defined by ordinary language dictionaries. Throughout, I have tried to strike the right balance, excluding the trivial and peripheral but providing relevant, durable and wherever possible quantitative information. Cross-references are made frequently but not haphazardly: they are used when necessary for the proper definition of a term, or when there is useful supplementary information (such as a figure) under a different heading to which attention should be drawn.

Units of measurement are covered in detail at the beginning of the book under the entry 'Units', with very little said under separate headings such as **therm** and **kilowatt**. Through the book SI units (the joule, the watt, etc.) have been used more or less consistently, with conversion factors available for other units. The names of world regions and countries do not occur in the main part of the dictionary; instead a special section on international energy statistics contains tabulated data for the 122 most populous nations.

Over four dozen figures and two dozen tables are included, almost all freshly designed or compiled for this dictionary. Deliberately, the figures have been used to illustrate less common concepts rather than to repeat the familiar images of the energy literature.

This dictionary's sources are legion, and I am indebted to the authors of innumerable books, journal articles and reports that I read before this work was conceived, or consulted since. Of the books, a small proportion are mentioned in the bibliography. I am very grateful to all the colleagues who have helped with information or assistance. I have benefited greatly from the facilities of Southampton University and the European Centre for Nuclear Research, and would also like to thank the Rutherford and Appleton Laboratories (UK Science and Engineering Research Council) and the United Nations (Geneva).

Units

In the field of energy, a wide and confusing range of units is in use among different professional groups, reflecting the diverse history of the subject and its importance in varied areas of work. The units in which energy itself is measured range in size from the electron volt up to the 'Q', and these differ by forty orders of magnitude.

One particular unit of energy, the joule, is accepted as standard by international convention; it has been adhered to as closely as possible elsewhere in this book. However, it would be quite unrealistic to imagine that the joule is universally understood or that one can avoid using other units such as Btu, quad, kilocalorie and so on as occasion demands.

Table A *Convention for the multiplication of units*

Multiplier	In words	Prefix	Abbr.
10^{18}	million million million	exa-	E
10^{15}	thousand million million	peta-	P
10^{12}	million million	tera-	T
10^{9}	thousand million	giga-	G
10^{6}	million	mega-	M
10^{3}	thousand	kilo-	k
10^{0}	the unit itself	no prefix	
10^{-3}	thousandth	milli-	m
10^{-6}	millionth	micro-	μ
10^{-9}	thousand millionth	nano-	n
10^{-12}	million millionth	pico-	p
10^{-15}	thousand million millionth	femto-	f
10^{-18}	million million millionth	atto-	a

Whatever is being measured, be it energy, power, length, mass, volume, etc., it is important to deal in a consistent way with large variations in magnitude. This is achieved by the system of prefixes given in Table A. For example, to express the power of a large electricity generating station it is much more convenient to write 1 gigawatt (1 GW) than 1,000,000,000 watts. The prefixes shown are now standard with the SI system of units (see Table D) and also occur with many non-standard units (e.g. MeV, TWh, Mtoe).

Units

Table B *Units of energy*

Abbr.	Name	Value
J	joule (standard SI unit of energy)	1.0 J
Btu	British thermal unit	1.055 kJ
cal	calorie	4.184 J
eV	electron volt	0.1602 aJ
erg	erg	100 nJ
kWh	kilowatt-hour	3.6 MJ
MWd	megawatt-day	86.4 GJ
Q	Q (1,000 quads)	1055.0 EJ
q	quad (a quadrillion Btu)	1.055 EJ
therm	(100,000 Btu)	105.5 MJ
thermie	(1,000,000 cal)	4.184 MJ

Table C *Units equivalent to energy*

Abbr.	Name	Value
amu	atomic mass unit	0.1492 nJ
bbl	barrel (of oil, 42 US galls)	6.15 GJ*
ft^3	cubic foot (of natural gas)	1.075 MJ*
Imp. gall.	Imperial gallon (of oil)	176.0 MJ*
kg	kilogram: mass equivalent	89.9 PJ
kg	kilogram: of natural uranium	0.34 TJ**
l	litre (of oil)	38.7 MJ*
m^3	cubic metre (of natural gas)	38.0 MJ*
m^3	cubic metre (of fuelwood)	15.25 GJ*
tce	tonne of coal equivalent	26.9 GJ*
toe	tonne of oil equivalent	44.8 GJ*
US gall	US gallon (of oil)	147.0 MJ*

*Approximate value, varying according to the quality of the fuel. For the tce and toe, there are differences between conventions.
**Typical value for electricity produced by a thermal reactor.

Table B summarises the units of energy in use and gives their values in joules; for some examples of energy magnitudes, see under **energy**.

In Table C are a number of units which in practice are equivalent to energy and which are used frequently in the appropriate industries. More information about calorific values is given under **fuels**.

Going beyond energy itself, physical quantities in general are best measured through the conventional SI system of units listed in Table D. This is built up out of fixed basic units (the metre for length, the kilogram for mass, etc.) so as to keep to a minimum the need for conversion factors when more complicated quantities (such as energy) are used. This is best illustrated by a counterexample: the kilowatt-hour (kWh) is a non-standard unit because it is based on the hour as unit of time,

Table D *SI units*

Name	Abbr.	Quantity measured	Dimensions
Basic units			
metre	m	length	—
kilogram	kg	mass	—
second	s	time	—
ampere	A	electric current	—
kelvin	K	temperature	—
mole	mol	no. of particles	—
candela	cd	luminous intensity	—
Derived units			
radian	rad	angle	none
steradian	sr	solid angle	none
hertz	Hz	frequency	s^{-1}
newton	N	force	$kg\ m\ s^{-2}$
pascal	Pa	pressure	$kg\ m^{-1}\ s^{-2}$
joule	J	energy	$kg\ m^2\ s^{-2}$
watt	W	power	$kg\ m^2\ s^{-3}$
coulomb	C	electric charge	$A\ s$
volt	V	potential	$kg\ m^2\ s^{-2}\ A^{-1}$
ohm	Ω	resistance	$kg\ m^2\ s^{-2}\ A^{-2}$
farad	F	capacitance	$kg^{-1}\ m^{-2}\ s^3\ A^2$
weber	Wb	magnetic flux	$kg\ m^2\ s^{-1}\ A^{-1}$
henry	H	inductance	$kg\ m^2\ s^{-1}\ A^{-2}$
tesla	T	magnetic induction	$kg\ s^{-1}\ A^{-1}$
becquerel	Bq	radioactivity	s^{-1}
gray	Gy	radiation dose	$m^2\ s^{-2}$
lumen	lm	luminous flux	$cd\ sr$
lux	lx	illumination	$cd\ sr\ m^{-2}$

instead of the second, in consequence of which the number of seconds in an hour (3,600) has to be brought into numerous calculations.

At the same time, it must be said that the SI system is far from perfect. It is confusing in that the unit of mass is prefixed (the kilogram, not the gram!), there are complications in expressing the energy in **electromagnetic** fields, and some of the SI units are still little used in comparison with older ones (e.g. the gray, cf. the rad.)

Table E contains miscellaneous conversion factors likely to be of particular use.

Table E *Miscellaneous conversions*

SI unit		Value in other units
1 metre	=	39.37 inches
1 kilometre	=	0.6214 miles
1 m^2	=	1,550 square inches
1 hectare	=	10,000 m^2 = 2.47 acres
1 m^3	=	0.0283 cubic feet = 220 Imp. gall. = 264 US gall.
1 kilogram	=	2.205 lb
1 tonne	=	1,000 kg = 1.102 tons
1 radian	=	57.3 degrees
1 newton	=	0.225 pounds weight
1 pascal	=	9.87 × 10^{-6} atmospheres
1 pascal	=	0.145 × 10^{-3} pounds weight per square inch
1 watt	=	0.00134 hp = 3.412 Btu/hour

Temperatures in Fahrenheit (F), Celsius (= centigrade, C), Kelvin (K), and Rankine (R):

$$9 \times (C + 40) = 5 \times (F + 40)$$
$$9 \times K = 5 \times R$$
$$K = C + 273.15$$

absolute zero   The lowest temperature to which any substance could conceivably be cooled, and at which it would contain no remaining energy in the form of heat. Absolute zero is close to −273 C and is by definition the zero of the Kelvin temperature scale (0 K).

absorption cycle   A thermodynamic cycle sometimes used to run heat pumps for refrigeration or air conditioning. Since it may be driven by heat energy rather than mechanical or electrical energy, the absorption cycle can be a useful alternative to the more familiar vapour compression cycle, and absorption cooling systems have been developed which run from solar heat and from industrial waste heat.

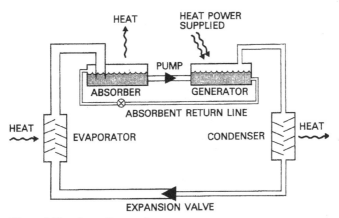

Figure 1 The absorption cycle.

The cycle makes use of two fluids, namely a refrigerant (which might be, for example, ammonia) and an absorbant (say, water). The right-hand side of Figure 1 is at high temperature and pressure, with the refrigerant condensing to give out heat; the left-hand side is at lower pressure and temperature so that heat is taken into an evaporator within the space being cooled. To complete the cycle, the evaporated refrigerant is allowed to dissolve in the absorbant and

5

is subsequently driven off from it again at higher pressure in another container (the generator) which is heated. The pump between the absorber and the generator expends very little energy (much less than the pump in a vapour compression cycle), most of the input power being the heat applied to the generator.

The absorption cycle can in practice give coefficients of performance (c.o.p.) of about one-third those possible with the vapour compression cycle, i.e. the c.o.p. is typically around unity. In circumstances where the generator heat is in effect free the absorption cycle is competitive and its technical development is progressing rapidly.

absorptivity (sometimes called absorptance, or absorptive power) When radiation falls onto a surface, some is reflected and some absorbed; the proportion absorbed is the absorptivity of the surface. It may vary according to the wavelength of the radiation, and so may be different between visible light and radiant heat. Absorptivity may also change somewhat with temperature.

The absorptivities of materials are valuable data for the design of buildings and rooms for energy efficiency and comfort. It can be shown that the absorptivity of a surface is equal to its **emissivity**, i.e. surfaces which are good at absorbing heat are also good at emitting it by radiation. For tabulated figures, see **emissivity**.

AC See **alternating current**.

accumulator (1) a **storage cell** which accumulates electrical energy in chemical form, i.e. a battery. The term 'accumulator' is used especially of lead-acid batteries such as those used in automobiles. (2) A reservoir of cooling water used in certain emergency core-cooling systems for nuclear reactors. The water is held under pressure in the accumulator and would automatically flow into the reactor core to cool it if there were a loss-of-coolant accident.

acetylene A gas (C_2H_2) which was often used as a fuel for lighting before electricity became widely available. It remains important in oxyacetylene burners for cutting and welding metals at temperatures which can exceed 3,000 C.

actinides The collective name given to a series of chemically similar metallic elements which includes those which are valuable for nuclear fission energy production and those sustaining, by radioactivity, the earth's internal heat.

The actinides are listed in Table 1, together with their atomic numbers and the range of mass numbers covered by the known isotopes of each actinide. For the most stable isotopes, the symbol and half-life are given.

Table 1 *The actinides*

Name	Atomic number	Mass numbers	Most stable isotope	
			Symbol	Half-life
actinium	89	227–228	^{227}Ac	22 years
thorium	90	227–234	^{232}Th	1.4×10^{10} years
protactinium	91	231–234	^{231}Pa	34,400 years
uranium	92	230–240	^{238}U	4.5×10^{9} years
neptunium	93	237–240	^{237}Np	2.1×10^{6} years
plutonium	94	238–244	^{244}Pu	8.3×10^{7} years
americium	95	241–244	^{243}Am	7,400 years
curium	96	242–249	^{247}Cm	1.6×10^{7} years
berkelium	97	243–250	^{247}Bk	1,400 years
californium	98	246–254	^{251}Cf	898 years
einsteinium	99	251–255	^{254}Es	276 days
fermium	100	250–257	^{257}Fm	82 days
mendelevium	101	255–257	^{257}Md	4 hours
nobelium	102	253–257	^{255}No	3 minutes
lawrencium	103	255–260	^{260}Lr	about 3 minutes

It is significant that the elements of higher mass number tend to be those with the shortest half-lives, i.e. to be the least stable. The only actinides sufficiently long-lived to be found in nature in large amounts are near the top of the table, i.e. thorium and uranium. All but these two are extremely rare or non-existent on the earth. Because of the heat of their radioactivity uranium and thorium are vital to the earth's overall energy balance and have had a powerful influence on long-term geophysical processes. The commercial significance of uranium and thorium reserves has been greatly enhanced by the roles which they may play in nuclear fission fuel cycles.

Several of the man-made actinides have found applications in industry, medicine and communications. Some, like americium, are used as sources of particular types of radiation in industry, while others such as californium provide radiotherapy. Others are used in isotopic power generators which produce electricity from decay heat and have been used to power satellites, navigation buoys, heart pacemakers and other devices for which regular fuelling is not possible.

Chemically, the actinides are mildly toxic, as are other heavy metals like lead and mercury. They are of special danger, however, because of the combined effect of (a) their radioactivity, and (b) their tendency when absorbed by the body to become concentrated in certain vital areas such as the bone marrow. This concentration means that relatively tiny amounts of, say, ^{239}Pu may cause serious illness by radiation damage to delicate organs or by carcinogenesis.

As a by-product of nuclear fission energy, dangerously large amounts of radioactive actinides are produced, and their disposal is one of the main technical difficulties for fission energy. A form of nuclear incineration has been proposed which could, in principle, reduce the dangerous actinides to safety within a relatively short time, but it is doubtful if this will be workable in the near future. See also **nuclear waste, transuranic elements.**

actinium A chemical element (atomic number $Z = 89$, symbol Ac) which is one of the group of elements known collectively as the **actinides.** Actinium occurs naturally in minute amounts, mainly the isotope ^{227}Ac, as part of the decay chain of uranium (^{235}U).

actinium series The series of **nuclides** which forms the decay chain of the nuclide ^{235}U down ultimately to ^{207}Pb (i.e. from uranium to lead). The mass numbers of the actinium series are of the general form $A = 4n + 3$, where n is an integer between 51 and 58 inclusive.

adenosine triphosphate (ATP) The organic substance which transfers the energy used for muscular contraction by animals. In the body of an average adult there will be about 75 g of ATP present at any instant of time, but the rate of production and consumption in the body tissues is such that he will actually use more like 75 kg of ATP per day, expending energy at a rate of about 150 W.

adiabatic When a system undergoes a process without any flow of heat out of the system, or into it, then the process is said to be adiabatic.

advanced gas-cooled reactor See **AGR.**

Advisory Committee on Reactor Safeguards (ACRS) A committee of the US Atomic Energy Commission, responsible for many years for recommendations on reactor safety.

AEC See **Atomic Energy Commission.**

aerodynamics The science of air flow across solid structures, fundamental to the design of aircraft and essential for the optimisation of automobiles, wind turbines and other devices. Proper attention to aerodynamics can make a 5-10 per cent difference to the energy efficiency of conventional automobiles by reducing the energy dissipated as air turbulence.

aerogenerator   See wind energy.

AGR   Advanced gas-cooled reactor. A type of nuclear reactor cooled by carbon dioxide gas in use in the UK.

agriculture   Economically and technologically, the development of agriculture is closely related to that of energy sources. Conventional agricultural efficiency depends on the use of tractors, artificial fertilisers, fresh water and transport for the distribution of produce, which demand energy resources unavailable in much of the Third World.

The growth of agriculture is leading to deforestation as fresh areas of the globe are cleared of virgin forests, and this may have widespread climatic effects in the long term. Agriculture is therefore closely inter-related with energy policy and with environment protection.

Agriculture contributes positively to the world's energy resources through biomass cultivation (see **biological energy**). Fuelwood is a familiar example, and **wood**, cultivated or otherwise, probably accounts for something like 10 per cent of world energy use. Future developments will probably centre on the production of high-grade liquid fuels from energy crops.

There have been many developments aimed at improving the energy systems of small agricultural communities in emergent nations, and the use of **biogas** generated from farmyard refuse and sewage has been of wide interest.

air   See atmosphere.

air battery   A type of electric **storage cell** in which one electrode is activated by the oxygen in the air.

air conditioning   The maintaining of the air in a building or vehicle at a temperature and composition comfortable for the occupants. It is essential for large buildings which are intensively used, such as industrial plants, and is of value not only for human comfort but also for enhancing the reliability and lifetime of machinery by providing a clean and stable working environment. Moreover, air conditioning is valuable for reasons of health, for example where perishable foodstuffs are stored.

Domestic air conditioning is common in climates where high temperatures or high humidity occur, and the energy demands of air conditioning systems in summer can be comparable to those for heating in winter. In countries such as the USA and India, units consuming 10 to 20 kW are not uncommon. In automobiles, a significant proportion of fuel consumption can go to power the air conditioning: 5 to 10 per cent is common in the USA.

In general, air conditioning consists of several stages. First, air drawn from within the building (or vehicle) is mixed with some fresh air from outside and is filtered to remove dust. To control humidity, moisture may be added to or removed from the air: in the latter case the air is cooled considerably to precipitate out the excess moisture. Before the air is recirculated, some final cooling or heating may be needed to achieve the desired temperature.

Because air conditioning is most needed under strong sunlight, it is recognised as an ideal application of solar energy, and numerous designs for solar air-conditioning systems have been made and tested. As energy prices in real terms rise, solar air conditioning may become increasingly competitive with electrically-powered units.

air mass   Solar radiation is attenuated by the atmosphere before reaching the earth's surface, to an extent dependent on the angle of the sun above the horizon. This dependence is measured by the 'air mass', defined as the ratio of the distance actually travelled by the radiation through the atmosphere to the distance vertically up through the atmosphere. 'Air mass zero' refers to radiation not attenuated at all by the atmosphere, i.e. to the full radiation from the sun in space. See also **solar constant**.

aircraft   In so far as energy efficiency has been a factor in traditional aircraft design, it has usually been to improve range rather than to reduce fuel costs. Only in the last few years have rising oil prices and increased competition among airlines forced the development of a new generation of commercial aircraft designed to carry large numbers of passengers cheaply, and it is now arguable that air travel on fully-laden aircraft consumes little or no more energy than alternative surface transport systems. See also **transport**.

albedo   The proportion of the incident solar light which is diffusely reflected from the atmosphere and surface of a planet back into space. The earth's albedo varies according to the patterns of vegetation and climate, and long-term variations in it may affect the planet's thermal stability. Its average value is about 0.3.

alcohol   The generic name given to a set of organic substances of which the simplest, chemically, is methyl alcohol (CH_3OH) and which includes also ethyl alcohol (CH_3CH_2OH) and propyl alcohol ($CH_3CH_2CH_2OH$). There are very many more complex alcohols, the general form being expressible as ROH where R is some hydrocarbon chain.

By international agreement ethyl alcohol is now more properly termed 'ethanol' and methyl alcohol 'methanol'. These are the most important alcohols economically, and ethanol in particular is the potable alcohol most readily fermented from agricultural produce. Alcohols fermented or extracted from biomass have frequently been suggested as potentially valuable energy sources, especially in parts of the world where fossil fuels are not locally obtainable and where there is arable land suited to the growing of an alcohol-producing crop. An example is the production, in Brazil, of manioc from which alcohol is derived and used as a transport fuel in admixture with gasoline. See also **fuel**.

alga (pl. algae) A form of microscopic aquatic plant life which has been proposed for use either as a fuel crop, i.e. as a way of photo-synthetically converting and storing solar energy, or as an organism for the biological conversion of sewage or other biological wastes into products which would include methane gas which could then be burnt as a fuel. See also **biological energy**.

alpha-decay A common form of radioactive decay for atomic nuclei, involving the emission by the nucleus of an alpha-particle, i.e. of a conglomerate of two protons and two neutrons, which is the same thing as a nucleus of the element helium. As an example of alpha-decay, the nucleus of common thorium (^{232}Th, having 90 protons and 142 neutrons) will decay in this way to yield a nucleus of radium, ^{228}Ra, which has 88 protons and 140 neutrons. Note that the mass number (the superscript to the element's symbol) is reduced by four units by alpha-decay.

For different **nuclides** alpha-decay occurs over widely differing time scales. In the case of thorium mentioned above the **half-life** is fourteen thousand million years, i.e. thorium decays away with extreme gradualness, which is why it is still an abundant element on the earth. By contrast, the nucleus of polonium ^{212}Po alpha-decays into lead (^{208}Pb) with a half-life of 0.3 microseconds, which is one reason why polonium is unfamiliar but lead is abundant. Whether or not a certain nuclide is liable to alpha-decay, and if so how quickly, are determined by the fine details of the nuclide's internal structure and needs to be found out by experiment. It turns out that alpha-decay is important for bismuth and the elements above it in atomic number, but is rather rare for lighter elements.

The stream of alpha-particles given off by a quantity of a decaying active substance is known as alpha-radiation. The particles have kinetic energies typically in the range 4-10 MeV (see 'Units') and will travel up to a few centimetres in air before being brought to rest. In solid materials the range is microscopic. Because the radiation does not penetrate far it is comparatively harmless unless the radioactive material finds its way actually into the body.

alternating current (AC)   An electric current which regularly changes its direction such that over a period there is no net flow of electric charge. Alternating current is the favoured method of transmitting electrical energy in a centralised distribution system. It is to be distinguished from **direct current (DC)** which may be provided by, for instance, storage cells.

By convention, AC normally alternates at a rate of 50 or 60 cycles per second, this variation in time being of sinusoidal form. See also **electricity**.

alternative technology   The form of technology which has been envisaged as an alternative to the so-called high technology which has spearheaded the development of the world's advanced nations in recent years. Alternative technology is thought of as a widely-disseminable set of skills and techniques permitting communities to live in prosperity and comfort without the environmental and social evils associated with large-scale centralised production and energy generation. Ideally, alternative technology is tailored to the special abilities and needs of the people concerned and to the opportunities they have for exploiting (but not degrading) their immediate environment. Examples of alternative technology include solar energy systems scaled to meet the demands of families or small villages; biogas producers which consume agricultural waste; and the generation of electricity in small amounts from windmills.

As a movement, alternative technology has been closely associated with the opposition to centralised electricity generation and in particular the opposition to nuclear power. It is likely to prove especially influential on the development strategies of a number of underdeveloped countries for whom progress along the pattern of the advanced nations is not a realistic objective.

alternator   see **generator**.

americium   The element of atomic number $Z = 95$, symbol Am. Americium is one of the **actinide** metals, and although it does not occur naturally in significant amounts the isotope ^{241}Am has been manufactured copiously from plutonium. That isotope is useful as a long-lived source of 60 keV gamma-radiation, for which purpose it has been exploited in the making of thickness gauges, fuel gauges, etc.

ammonia   A liquid (chemically, NH_3) with melting and boiling points somewhat lower than those of water. Ammonia finds wide application as a refrigerant: see, for example, **absorption cycle**.

ampere   The unit of measurement of a flow of **electricity**. One ampere is equal to a flow of 1 coulomb per second, and 1 coulomb is the electric charge on 6.25×10^{18} protons. An ampere is typical of the current through, say, an ordinary light bulb.

amu   Atomic mass unit.

anaerobic digestion   The decomposition of organic material by micro-organisms, without oxygenation, usually producing methane. In chemical terms the process goes something like

$$C_6H_{10}O_5 + H_2O \rightarrow 3CO_2 + 3CH_4$$

but this is a simple representation of what is a complex multi-stage process. Moreover, in any system there will be several micro-organisms active at once. See also **biological energy**.

anemometer   A device for measuring or indicating the speed of the wind.

angström   An obsolescent unit of distance, equal to 10^{-10} metre, used especially to refer to wavelengths of light. See also 'Units'.

annihilation   A term used loosely to describe the conversion of mass into radiant or thermal energy, usually in the context of particle physics or cosmology. For example, the universe is filled with radiant energy which is believed to have come from the annihilation of matter in the very early history of the universe.

anode   One of the two terminals of a DC electrical device such as a storage cell, electroplating cell or electron tube. Current flows into the device through the anode (i.e. electrons flow out) and current flows out through the other terminal, the cathode.

antimatter   Just as ordinary matter is composed out of certain types of **particles**, so the corresponding **antiparticles** could conceivably

13

form an opposed antimatter. Antimatter and matter could not co-exist in contact, because mutual annihilation would occur with intense production of radiant energy. Therefore antimatter is not found to exist naturally on the earth. In distant galaxies, however, the opposite may be the case, i.e. there may be antimatter but no matter; the amount of antimatter in the universe is an important issue in cosmological theories but is at the moment very uncertain.

antineutrino   The antiparticle of the **neutrino**, an antineutrino may be emitted from a nucleon when it undergoes beta-decay. Neutrons, for example, which are produced copiously in the cores of nuclear fission reactors, decay into protons with the emission of electrons and antineutrinos.

antiparticle   The elementary particles which make up the universe form a rich variety of types, and these types are characterised by a small number of parameters such as mass, angular momentum, electric charge, baryon number and strangeness. Some of the values, including mass and angular momentum, are always positive numbers, but others may take on negative as well as positive values. These 'additive quantum numbers' include electric charge. For any particle, the corresponding antiparticle is that which is specified when the additive quantum numbers are changed in sign. A fundamental theorem tells us that the workings of physics are symmetric between particle and antiparticle.

For example, the proton (i.e. nucleus of hydrogen, ^{1}H) has as its antiparticle the antiproton, the latter having the same mass and stability as the proton but a negative electric charge and baryon number. The antiparticle of the antiproton is the proton.

A small proportion of particles have zero electric charge, zero baryon number, etc., and so do not have distinct antiparticles. This is the case for the photon. In many contexts it is unnecessary to distinguish between particles and antiparticles, and both are referred to by the name of the former. Thus, when discussing radioactivity, 'electron' may refer either to the electron itself or to its antiparticle the positron, and 'neutrino' embraces 'antineutrino'.

ash   Solid residue, left after the burning of a fuel either because of impurities in the fuel or because combustion was incomplete. In the latter case coal or oil ash may contain a good deal of carbon; otherwise it may contain a variety of minerals in oxide and hydroxide form, such as potassium and calcium. Many types of ash are useful as fertilisers.

Athabasca   An area in Canada well known for its extensive **tar sands** deposits.

atmosphere   The earth's atmosphere is a highly complex system which interacts with, and modifies, geological and biological processes on the surface and the solar radiation from above. Its composition has evolved over the life of the earth and is changing now in response to the activities of man.

The atmosphere is now primarily composed of nitrogen (N_2, 78% by volume) and oxygen (O_2, 21%). The third largest component is argon (Ar), a gas which is not chemically reactive but which has some relevance to nuclear energy since the argon nucleus can be activated by a neutron to form the radioactive isotope ^{41}Ar, which decays with a half-life of 110 minutes.

The bulk of the atmosphere is contained within a layer known as the troposphere, extending from the bottom of the atmosphere up to a height of the order of a dozen kilometres. Above it, increasingly more rarefied layers extend hundreds of kilometres farther up, shading off into 'inner' space. The atmosphere has a mass of about 5,000 exagrams, i.e. about one-millionth that of the earth as a whole. This mass gives a pressure of 101,325 pascals at sea level. The atmosphere blows about with a kinetic energy that probably totals several hundred exajoules, an amount similar to the total annual world energy consumption. See also **wind energy**.

The troposphere is heated from below, largely through the absorption of infra-red radiation by **carbon dioxide** (CO_2), a gas which amounts to a tiny proportion of the atmosphere (about 0.03% by volume) but on which biological processes and climatic stability depend critically. Man's activities have already increased the atmosphere's CO_2 content considerably, and continued deforestation and fossil-fuel combustion may have very damaging effects, including a substantial rise in the average temperature.

Another constituent of the atmosphere, minute as a proportion but vital in its significance, is water vapour. Water in the form of clouds has an obvious climatic significance, and the deposition of rain and snow on land drives the 'water cycle' without which hydro-electric power, not to mention agriculture, would not exist. The atmosphere is kept moist by evaporation from the oceans, which takes place at a rate dependent on temperature and so is inter-related with the CO_2 level.

Trace amounts of other gases are also present in the atmosphere, e.g. methane, carbon monoxide, and oxides of nitrogen and sulphur. Some, such as sulphur dioxide, are pollutants given off by processes

15

such as coal-burning. Moreover, the atmosphere contains particles of dust, ash and salt which may be significant in cloud formation and precipitation. In the past, there have been times when volcanic activity led to sharp increases in the amounts of ash and dust in the air; now, artificial sources are of more concern.

The higher reaches of the atmosphere, above the troposphere, are tenuous but have an important role to play in the absorbing of ultra-violet (UV) radiation from the sun. In particular, oxygen in both its molecular forms (O_2 and ozone, O_3) prevents damage to life by blocking off UV radiation while permitting longer wavelengths (visible light) to penetrate to the earth's surface. This has the result that the atmosphere is heated to high temperatures at great height, a reversal of the state of affairs in the troposphere where temperature falls as height increases.

Being sensitive to the solar radiation spectrum, and also to the flow of charged particles from the sun (the 'solar wind') the upper atmosphere can act to bring about climatic change on the earth in response to changes in the sun itself.

atom An atom is one of the tiny structures out of which ordinary matter is built up. It has a core, or nucleus, consisting of a number of nucleons, i.e. neutrons and protons. The number of protons, which may range from one up to about a hundred, fixes the kind of chemical element the atom belongs to. The number of neutrons is usually somewhat larger than that of the protons, and for any particular element it is variable over a small range of values which correspond to the different **isotopes** the element may have. The nucleons are themselves complex structures, but can be thought of as dense and stable objects with a size of about 1 femtometre. The atomic nucleus, being formed of close-packed nucleons, has a size ranging up to several fm.

Protons have an electrical charge which is positive, and so therefore do atomic nuclei. The nuclei attract an accretion of negatively charged particles, i.e. electrons, and the resulting neutral structure is the complete atom. However, electrons are very much lighter than nucleons, and the electrical attraction which binds them is much more feeble than the nuclear force which binds the nucleons into the nucleus: consequently, the electrons are widely separated from the nucleus and spread over a comparatively large volume of space. Exactly why the electron is so light, and why the nuclear and electrical forces have such different strengths, are questions to which there are still no satisfactory answers.

For illustrative purposes, some masses and sizes are indicated in Table 2. Note that the nucleus is more dense than the atom as a

Table 2 *Atomic masses and sizes*

Object	Mass (kg)	Radius
Nucleon (p or n)	1.7×10^{-27}	0.7 fm
Electron (e)	0.9×10^{-30}	2.8 fm
Nucleus of iron (26p + 30n)	95×10^{-27}	4.6 fm
Hydrogen atom (p + e)	1.7×10^{-27}	0.10 nm
Iron atom (26p + 30n + 26e)	95×10^{-27}	0.16 nm

whole by several orders of magnitude, a fact which underlies the unusual potential of nuclear energy.

Atomic Energy Commission (AEC) US government body originally responsible for nuclear energy. In 1976 its functions were divided between the Energy Research and Development Administration (ERDA) and the Nuclear Regulatory Commission (NRC).

atomic number The number (Z) of protons in the nucleus of an atom; it determines the element to which the atom belongs, and therefore the chemical properties which will be manifested by the substance. The simplest element, hydrogen, has atomic number $Z = 1$; the next element is helium with $Z = 2$; and so on up through heavier elements like iron ($Z = 26$) to very heavy ones like uranium ($Z = 92$).

automobile See **transport**.

Avogadro's number (symbol N_A) Reflects the enormous number of atoms in an everyday quantity of any substance. It is defined as the number of carbon (^{12}C) atoms in an amount of that isotope weighing 12 grams. For any isotope of any element, it is approximately the number of atoms in a mass in grams equal to the atomic mass number, e.g. in 1 gram of hydrogen or in 56 grams of iron. Avogadro's number is equal to 6.02×10^{23}.

barrel (bbl) A common measure of quantity of oil, equal to 159 litres and corresponding approximately to 130 kg in weight. In energy terms, 1 bbl = 6.15 GJ or thereabouts, according to the exact composition of the oil.

baryon   In nuclear physics this is the collective name given to the types of heavy particle of which the proton and the neutron are the most relevant examples. A baryon is a bound system of three quarks. Baryons are 'conserved' in the sense that no kind of nuclear reaction can destroy them, a fact which is reflected in the way that the mass numbers must balance in the formula for any reaction. For example, in the decay of uranium $^{238}U \rightarrow {}^{234}Th + {}^{4}He$, we have $238 = 234 + 4$.

baseload   In any large-scale electricity supply system, it is useful to distinguish between the constant energy demand, which must be met continuously, and the varying demand, changing from hour to hour and day to day, which must be met flexibly. The former of these is the baseload.

bbl   See **barrel**.

becquerel   The SI unit of radioactivity, more correct (but much less commonly used) than the **curie**. A sample of material with an average of 1 radioactive disintegration per second corresponds to 1 becquerel (1 Bq).

benzene   A highly flammable liquid (C_6H_6). An important fuel in the chemical industry. Can be manufactured from petroleum or coal.

berkelium   The element of atomic number $Z = 97$, symbol Bk; one of the **actinide** metals.

beryllium   A light metal which acts as an excellent moderator for neutrons within a nuclear fission reactor. It is used either in pure metallic form, or as an oxide, or (in the **MSBR**) as a molten fluoride salt, BeF_2.

beta-decay   The process by which a neutron may transform itself into a proton with the emission of an electron and an antineutrino. The term is also used to describe the reverse process when a proton is transformed into a neutron together with a positive electron (positron) and a neutrino; this reverse process is comparatively unusual and can occur only in certain proton-rich nuclides.

   An example of beta-decay is furnished by the potassium isotope ^{40}K, which is responsible for a substantial part of the earth's natural radioactivity and which decays into calcium with a **half-life** of 1.26×10^9 years. The ^{40}K nucleus contains 19 protons and 21 neutrons, and the decay converts a neutron into a proton to form the stable calcium isotope ^{40}Ca. There is an electron released with an energy of about 1 MeV (160 fJ) from each decaying nucleus. The stream of electrons given off by a quantity of 'beta-active' material is known as 'beta-radiation', and is potentially dangerous to life. The neutrinos or antineutrinos are in this respect irrelevant.

Beta-active materials are a cause of concern when there is a likelihood of their being ingested into the body and becoming concentrated in organs which could then be damaged by ensuing beta-radiation.

Betz formula   No windmill can be 100 per cent efficient, in the sense of absorbing all the energy of the wind which passes through it. If it were, it would mean that the wind was being slowed down to rest leaving no remaining energy of motion in the air; and that would mean that there was no room for more air to pass through the windmill. This limitation is expressed by the Betz formula, which states that the maximum theoretical efficiency of a windmill is equal to 16/27, i.e. about 59 per cent. It is derived by applying the Bernouilli equation of hydrodynamics.

bicycle   A man-powered vehicle permitting transport at an energy cost of about 400 J m^{-1} for a person of average size, i.e. one-fifth of the energy cost of travel on foot. This is achieved by reducing frictional dissipation, and at the cost of a network of smooth, low-gradient roads and paths. See also **transport**.

binding energy   When a force pulls two or more objects together, energy is released; to pull them apart again an equal amount of energy would have to be reinjected into the system. That amount is known as the 'binding energy' of the system. For the nuclear force, which binds nucleons into atomic nuclei, binding energies can approach the einsteinian equivalent of 1 per cent of the mass of material. For example, a middle-range element like iron has a nuclear binding energy of about 0.8 PJ kg^{-1}. By contrast, much smaller binding energies apply to weaker forces such as the gravitational force: the earth's gravitational binding energy around the sun is equal to the nuclear binding energy of one-millionth part of the earth.

Figure 2 shows the nuclear binding energies per kilogram of various nuclides in a plot against their mass numbers. It is also given in the more conventional units of MeV per nucleon. The fact that the binding energy is generally lower for smaller nuclides means that energy can in principle be released by letting them fuse together into larger nuclides, and this is the basis of nuclear fusion power. How-

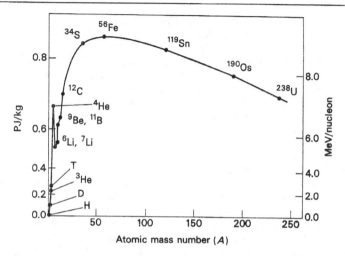

Figure 2 Nuclear binding energies. The energy per kilogram, or per nucleon, is shown against the total number of nucleons in the nucleus (*A*).

ever, the elements of very high mass number behave differently, with the binding energy per nucleon slowly falling off with increasing mass number. It is because of this circumstance that energy can be released by splitting nuclides with mass numbers at the top end of the range into halves (nuclear fission).

bioconversion   The conversion of one substance into another by biological action, e.g. the fermentation of carbohydrates into alcohol. See also **biological energy**.

biogas   A combustible fuel gas, mainly methane, produced by the controlled decomposition of organic wastes. See also **biological energy**.

biogeneration   A term sometimes used for the organic production of fuels. See also **biological energy**.

biological energy   A variety of biological systems can be used for the production or conversion of energy other than as food. They may be classified into:

(a) photosynthesis, by which solar energy is converted into carbohydrates such as cellulose or sugar;

(b) anaerobic fermentation, by which plant biomass may be converted by micro-organisms into alcohol; and

(c) Enzymatic breakdown or digestion of biomass with the production of methane gas.

The most promising schemes consist of the cultivation of a carefully selected crop, fermentation or digestion into a convenient fuel, and integration into an existing agricultural tradition. Innumerable crops have been proposed, and what follows is no more than a 'sampler' of a few current ideas.

Algae It has long been recognised that marine or estuarine algae can be harvested to provide valuable **biomass**. To yield fuels there are certain species which contain a large proportion of combustible hydrocarbon oil, e.g. *Alga bolrycoccus braunii* with oil amounting up to 65 per cent of its dry weight.

Babassu is a natural palm tree which grows in northern and central Brazil and the neighbouring part of Bolivia. In particular, it has thrived on land in north-eastern Brazil which had been cleared in the past for other purposes such as the nineteenth-century cotton industry. There are two species, *Orbignya martiniana* and *O. oleifera*.

The babassu 'coconuts' consist of a fibrous epicarp which can yield charcoal, a mesocarp which is starchy and can be fermented into alcohol and a less useful wood-like endocarp within. However, the endocarp has embedded in it a number of oil-bearing nuts (largest in the *O. oleifera* variety) which are useful as food, for soap-making, and many other purposes. In fact, it is on account of the oil-bearing nuts rather than as an energy source that babassu has come to be gathered on a large scale in Brazil.

Babassu has the advantages of growing wild, providing widespread casual employment, and giving an internationally saleable product (high quality vegetable oil) as well as energy in the forms of alcohol and charcoal.

Grain production as food leads unavoidably to a certain amount of spoiled grain which is unfit for eating but can be fermented into alcohol. A scheme in Nebraska, USA, is expected to yield about 20 million gallons of alcohol annually from this source, and the alcohol will be added to gasoline to give 'gasohol'.

Kelp. The Giant Kelp (*Macrocystis pyrifera*) is a marine plant which grows rapidly 10 or 15 metres below the ocean surface. Cultivated on artificial rafts at that depth, the kelp can yield biomass at a rate far greater than any terrestrial plant, with methane as a possible fuel to be produced from the kelp by enzymatic breakdown. Besides energy, there are food products which could also be made.

Manioc is a plant with starchy tuberous roots, a native of central Brazil, with a long history as a food crop. It appears under a variety of names, e.g. aipim, cassava, mandioca, yucca and tapioca. There is a bitter variety containing some hydrocyanic acid, and a sweet manioc without the acid content but also with less starch. Since alcohol can readily be fermented from the starch of the roots, manioc is a promising energy crop.

Molasses. A by-product of the sugar industry, molasses is often available very cheaply in parts of the world which lack local fossil-fuel resources. Conversion into alcohol by fermentation, for use as a vehicle fuel, is an attractive possibility.

Rubber. The rubber plant (*Hevea*) is another well-known crop which could find a new use as a source of alcohol through fermentation.

Wastes. Specially selected crops are not always necessary for the production of biological fuels; in some circumstances mixed agricultural wastes may profitably be used in this way. The most celebrated development of this kind is the use of methane-producing digesters in China, and especially in Szechwan. Vegetable matter and animal wastes are input, and energy (methane) and fertiliser are output. As an incidental bonus, improved sanitation is achieved.

Water Hyacinth. This shallow-water plant, *Eichornia crasspipes*, grows with great speed in warm nutrient-rich water such as that of tropical rivers and estuaries. As much as 300 kg m^{-2} of growth can be yielded annually, corresponding to about 20 kg of dry matter which can be converted into methane for fuel.

Wood. The most familiar biological fuel is firewood, and it still accounts for something like 10 per cent of the world's energy consumption. Uncontrolled wood-gathering can be economically and environmentally disastrous, but properly managed it can be an acceptable and sustainable source of power. Wood consumption as a fuel amounts to about a thousand million tonnes annually, or 0.6 TW. Most of this is consumed in the southern hemisphere; as much again is produced in the north, but for construction and paper-making rather than as fuel.

There are certain points which need to be made concerning biological energy in general. One is that the conversion of biomass into a fuel is a process with substantial leeway for choice in the organisms which are to be used and the nature of the fuel: there are schemes which would give methane and alcohol as well, different kinds of alcohol are possible, and there are yeasts which will give other products such as acetone and butanol.

Another common theme is the 'marginality' of biological energy production. Energy production may be peripheral to another, more lucrative, use of the primary crop; or it may use land which would not be available if it could be farmed economically for food; or it may go towards marginally reducing an existing dependence on fossil fuels. This is not to say that biological energy is not worthwhile, but it does mean that any proposed system must be assessed in its full context.

Finally, it must be remarked that biological energy may be as damaging to the environment as any other kind of energy industry. In the growing of the crop, soil deterioration must be prevented just as in the case of intensive food-growing, and in the burning of the fuel atmospheric pollution is a possibility. It is a good feature (by contrast with fossil fuels) that biological fuels will not raise atmospheric carbon-dioxide levels if the fuel crop is cultivated on otherwise unused ground.

biomass A general term for biological material, living or dead, but excluding that which has become fossilised or completely broken down chemically. (For global quantities, see Figure 5, under **carbon cycle**.)

bitumen Natural flammable liquid hydrocarbons, ranging in texture from near-solids like asphalt to petroleums; but the term is often reserved for the near-solid hydrocarbons. Bitumen is found naturally within crude oil, within coal ('bituminous' coal), within inorganic shales (bituminous shales) and occasionally alone.

black body A term in thermodynamics, referring to a body whose surface absorbs all the electromagnetic radiation incident upon it. It is an abstraction, but one which permits the calculation of quantities such as the amount of heat given off by an object at any particular temperature. In practice all surfaces differ somewhat from exact black-body behaviour, but the differences can be taken into account by introducing factors such as **emissivity** or **albedo**. See also **Stefan–Boltzmann law**.

BNFL British Nuclear Fuels Limited, the company which controls the fabrication and reprocessing of nuclear fuel in the UK.

boiling water reactor (BWR) See **nuclear reactors**.

boron A light element (atomic number $Z = 5$, symbol B) which has the property of absorbing neutrons readily and so can be used in the control of nuclear fission reactors. One isotope of boron, ^{11}B, may be useful in the future as a nuclear fusion fuel.

Brayton cycle A thermodynamic cycle which is the principle of operation of the gas turbine. The cycle is illustrated in Figure 3, showing the way the pressure and volume of the gas are changed. The steps are (1) the isentropic compression of a fuel-rich gas, (2)

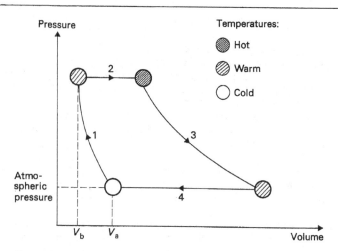

Figure 3 The Brayton cycle.

its heating by combustion at constant pressure, (3) its further expansion through an expansion turbine to give mechanical power, and (4) the discharge of the warm exhaust, fresh air and fuel being taken in again.

The efficiency of the Brayton cycle can in theory be as much as

$$\eta = 1 - V_b/V_a$$

where the ratio V_b/V_a is the compression ratio.

breeder   A nuclear reactor which is designed to 'breed' new nuclear fuel, perhaps as well as producing useful heat in its own right. Breeding is brought about by the irradiation by neutrons of a suitably chosen 'fertile' substance in the reactor core or in a 'blanket' surrounding it. A single neutron can convert a fertile nucleus into a fissile one; but since the fission chain reaction will sometimes give a net release of more than one neutron per fission, there is the possibility of breeding more fuel than is actually fissioned in the reactor.

Three breeder reactions are of interest:

(a) Plutonium breeding, which offers the prospect of utilising the non-fissile isotope of natural uranium, ^{238}U. The process is as follows:

$$n + \quad ^{238}U \rightarrow \ ^{239}U$$
$$^{239}U \rightarrow \ ^{239}Np + e^- \text{ (beta-decay)}$$
$$^{239}Np \rightarrow \ ^{239}Pu + e^- \text{ (beta-decay)}$$

To achieve this the neutrons need to be 'fast' ones, not moderated in energy after having been produced through fission. The two beta-decay transitions have half-lives of 24 minutes (into neptunium) and 57 hours (into plutonium).

(b) The thorium cycle, by which a new fissile isotope of uranium, not otherwise occurring in nature, can be produced out of thorium:

$$n + {}^{232}Th \rightarrow {}^{233}Th$$
$${}^{233}Th \rightarrow {}^{233}Pa + e^- \text{ (beta-decay)}$$
$${}^{233}Pa \rightarrow {}^{233}U + e^- \text{ (beta-decay)}$$

Here, the two beta-decays through protactinium into uranium have half-lives of 22 minutes and 27 days respectively. The thorium cycle is convenient in that the neutrons used need not be 'fast', and so conventional thermal reactors could be used for breeding in this way without the need for specially designed 'fast breeders'.

(c) A heavy isotope of hydrogen, tritium (^{3}H) is potentially valuable as a 'fusible' nuclear fuel. It does not occur readily in nature because of its short half-life (12 years) but can be bred out of the metal lithium:

$$n + {}^6Li \rightarrow {}^3H + {}^4He$$

The other product is ordinary inert helium, ^{4}He. Although tritium is a fusion fuel, there is no reason why it should not be bred in a fission reactor.

A number of different reactor designs have appeared in which breeding may be exploited; see also **nuclear reactors, nuclear fuel cycles**.

British thermal unit (Btu)   A measure of heat energy equal to 1,056 J. See 'Units'.

brown coal   Otherwise known as lignite, a fossil fuel of relatively low energy content (about 14 MJ/kg). There are substantial reserves of lignite but with wide variations in quality. See also **fuel**.

burner   In nuclear engineering, a reactor designed to produce heat by fission without also acting as a breeder of fuel.

burn-up   The specific burn-up of fuel in a nuclear reactor is the total amount of heat released per kilogram of the fuel, conventionally given in megawatt days per kilogram (MWD/kg). The 'burn-up' may alternatively mean the percentage of fissile nuclei in the fuel which the reactor succeeds in fissioning.

butane   A hydrocarbon (C_4H_{10}) obtained from crude oil and sometimes marketed in pressurised liquid form. It is a gas at normal pressure and so is a convenient cooking fuel.

BWR Boiling water reactor. See **nuclear reactors**.

cadmium A metallic element (atomic number $Z = 48$, symbol Cd) potentially useful in electrochemical cells such as the nickel-cadmium storage cell and the cadmium sulphide photovoltaic cell. Cadmium also has an application in the nuclear industry, its readiness to absorb neutrons making it ideal in control rods which can quench the nuclear chain reaction.

caesium A metallic element (atomic number $Z = 55$) one of whose isotopes, ^{137}Cs, is a radioactive fission product of uranium. The half-life of ^{137}Cs is some 30 years.

calandria A network of pipes running through the core of a nuclear reactor so as to bring a working fluid (coolant and/or moderator) into close proximity to all parts of the core. The term is best known with regard to the **CANDU** reactor design.

Calder Hall The site in Cumbria where, in 1956, the world's first nuclear power reactor (as opposed to experimental or purely military reactors) began to produce electricity. The Calder Hall reactors were also intended to produce plutonium.

californium The element of atomic number $Z = 98$, symbol Cf, one of the **actinide** metals. The most useful isotope is ^{252}Cf, which decays occasionally by spontaneous fission and thereby is an intense source of neutrons which sustains itself for a number of years. This has been applied to radiotherapy.

calorie A unit of energy equal to 4.184 J. The calorie is defined as the heat energy needed to raise the temperature of 1 gram of water by 1 Celsius degree. In medicine and zoology 'Calorie' (usually capitalised) actually means a kilocalorie, i.e. 4185 J.

calorific value   The amount of heat energy given by the combustion of a fuel per unit of mass or volume. For example, kerosine has a calorific value of about 48 MJ/kg (megajoules per kilogram).

calorimetry   The measurement of heat energy and its flow.

cancer   Forms of this disease may be caused by the absorption of certain chemical pollutants into the body or by radioactivity. Chemical and radiological carcinogens are certainly produced by the energy industries and in the case of nuclear power may well be the dominant constraint on the industry. On the other hand, it remains true today that there are many non-energy-related sources of carcinogens in developed societies and many natural sources.

CANDU   The Canadian deuterium–uranium reactor; see **nuclear reactors**.

Capenhurst   The site, in Cheshire, of Britain's gaseous diffusion plant for the making of highly enriched uranium suitable for military purposes. More recently an international collaboration involving Britain, Germany and the Netherlands has begun gas centrifuge enrichment work at Capenhurst for peaceful purposes.

carbodydrates   Substances formed from carbon, hydrogen and oxygen with the general chemical formula $C_m(H_2O)_n$. They are the principal product of plant **photosynthesis** and (as cellulose) form the bulk of living plant matter. Carbohydrates are the point of origin for a number of fuels such as alcohol (by fermentation), coal (by fossilisation) and fats (by bioconversion within animals). See also **biological energy**.

carbon   The element of atomic number $Z = 6$, occurring predominantly as the isotope ^{12}C. The earth's primeval carbon may have been in the form of carbon dioxide, methane and the like, but the processes associated with the evolution and elaboration of life have eliminated almost all the carbon from the atmosphere and trapped it in fossil hydrocarbons and carbonate rocks. Carbon is a universal constituent of organic material, and an ingredient of most everyday fuels. Charcoal and coke are valuable high-temperature fuels consisting of nearly pure carbon.
    In nuclear engineering, carbon finds application in control rods because of its property of easily absorbing neutrons.

carbon cycle   The natural flow of carbon between the atmosphere,

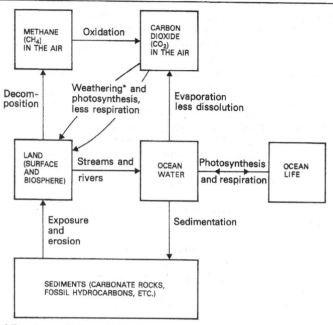

* E.g. the weathering and dissolution of carbonate rocks,

$$CaCo_3 + CO_2 + H_2O \rightarrow Ca^{++} + 2.HCO_3^-$$

Figure 4 Natural flows of carbon.

the oceans, the biosphere and sedimentary rocks. These reservoirs of carbon are displayed in Figure 4, which indicates the processes at work in the carbon cycle. Figure 5 gives quantitative information, including estimates of the amounts of carbon involved. However, this natural cycle has been greatly modified by man's activities; the extraction and burning of fossil carbon (the fossil fuels), and the loss of land biomass through forest clearances, are transferring several gigatonnes per year of carbon into the air. Much of this may be soaked up into the oceans, but there is a large amount accumulating in the atmosphere and leading to a continuing rise in its carbon-dioxide content (Figure 6).

carbon dioxide is a gas, with chemical composition CO_2, accounting naturally for a very small proportion of the atmosphere, i.e. less than 300 parts per million by volume. Figure 7 shows how this proportion has risen in recent years and will certainly continue to

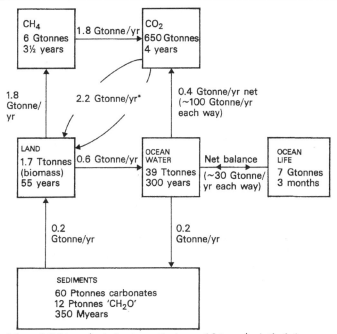

* Some 0.2 Gtonne/yr is due to weathering, and 2 tonne/yr is the balance of photosynthesis over respiration.

Figure 5 Quantities of carbon and residence times. For each natural reservoir, the total mass of carbon is given, albeit with large uncertainties in some cases. The flows in and out of each, and the average residence times, correspond to the 'natural' pre-industrial world.

rise through oil-, gas- and coal-burning. In itself carbon dioxide is harmless to animals and beneficial to plants, which use it in **photosynthesis**; but an increasing amount in the atmosphere will have climatic consequences through the **greenhouse effect**.

carbon monoxide (CO)   A kind of partially-oxidised carbon given off as a gas in small quantities whenever hydrocarbon fuels are burnt. It is particularly prevalent in automobile exhausts. Besides being a waste of energy (since it arises from incomplete combustion), carbon monoxide is toxic, blocking the take-up of oxygen by the blood by forming a compound, carboxyhaemoglobin, in the red blood cells. Its toxicity is compounded by the fact that it is undetectable by smell.

29

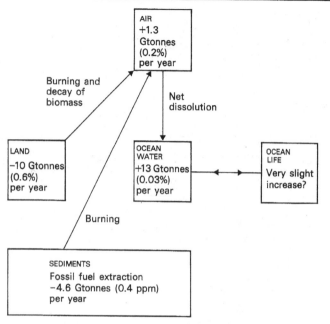

Figure 6 Changes to the natural carbon cycle. The approximate amounts of carbon building up in, or being taken from, each natural reservoir are estimated.

Carnot cycle   An idealised **thermodynamic cycle** for a heat engine, by which a volume of gas is alternately compressed, heated and allowed to expand, and compressed again, so that heat energy may be converted into mechanical work. The cycle (Figure 8) is illustrated both in terms of pressure and volume and in terms of temperature and entropy. The steps are (1) isentropic compression, (2) constant-temperature heat input, (3) isentropic expansion, and (4) constant-temperature heat rejection.

The Carnot cycle is best understood by introducing the concept of entropy as in the lower part of the figure; it can then be shown that the maximum efficiency of the cycle (the ratio of mechanical power out to heat energy in) is

$$\eta = 1 - T_a/T_b.$$

The fact that this depends only on the ratio of the absolute temperatures around the cycle has important consequences for heat pumps and heat engines in general.

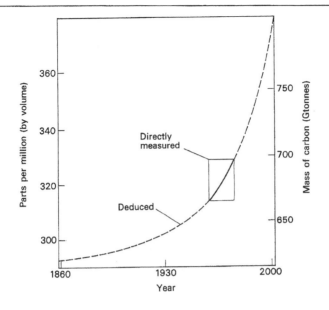

Figure 7 The build-up of carbon dioxide in the atmosphere, 1860–2000. (From L. Machta, 'The role of the oceans and biosphere in the carbon dioxide cycle', in D. Dyrssen and D. Jagner (eds), *The Changing Chemistry of the Oceans*, Wiley Interscience, New York, 1972).

cassava   Is known also as 'manioc' and by several other names. A tuberous plant commonly cultivated in countries such as Brazil and having potential value as a fuel crop. See also **biological energy**.

cathode   See **anode**.

CEA   The Commissariat d'Energie Atomique, the French governmental body responsible for nuclear power.

CEGB   The Central Electricity Generating Board, which is responsible in the United Kingdom for the non-nuclear generation of electricity and for the marketing and distribution of electricity.

cellulose   The carbohydrate forming the bulk of most plant material, including wood. It can be used as input to certain **biological energy** conversion systems or used as a fuel in its own right, having a calorific value of around 14 MJ/kg.

31

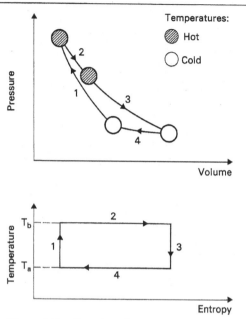

Figure 8 The Carnot cycle.

Celsius The degree Celsius (abbr. to C) is a conventional unit of temperature. Water freezes at 0 C, a comfortable room-temperature is 20 C, normal blood-temperature is near 37 C, and water boils at 100 C.

centigrade A synonym of **celsius**, the latter now being the favoured term in many countries.

cesium The American spelling of **caesium**.

chain reaction The process by which nuclear fission, induced by neutrons, leads to the release of yet more neutrons which cause yet more **fission**. This will occur within a quantity of the lighter natural uranium isotope, ^{235}U, or within plutonium (^{239}Pu), or within the artificial uranium isotope (^{233}U) which can be 'bred' out of thorium. A chain reaction will begin spontaneously, since there are always a few neutrons present—released, for example, through the action of cosmic rays. The chain reaction will build up if the fissile material (^{235}U, ^{239}Pu or ^{233}U) is in sufficient quantity and contained in a compact volume. An uncontrolled chain reaction amounts to a nuclear explosion; a controlled chain reaction is the basis of a **nuclear reactor**.

Chalk River The site in Quebec province, Canada, of a research centre where Canada's first nuclear reactors were built in the late 1940s.

charcoal See **carbon**.

chemical energy A general term for energy associated with the chemical bonds which link atoms into the familiar substances of everyday life. Since those bonds are electromagnetic in origin, chemical energy is a form of electromagnetic energy, different in kind from nuclear or gravitational energy.

chemical heat pump A kind of heat pump based on chemical potentials. A simple example (Figure 9) is provided by containers of pure water and of concentrated sulphuric acid, linked by a pipe above the liquid surfaces. Water vapour will flow from the one to the other, and the sulphuric acid container will be at an enhanced temperature; heat is thereby transferred across the system and upgraded to a higher temperature. A practical, self-sustaining system would be rather more complex, such as that shown in Figure 10. This consists of (a) a water reservoir containing pure cool water, taking in low-grade heat from, for example, a cheap solar collector; (b) a vapour absorption reservoir, taking up vapour from the water reservoir and so heating up the sulphuric acid solution which it contains; (c) a storage reservoir into which fluid from the vapour

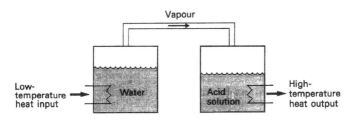

Figure 9 A simple chemical heat pump. (After P. F. Smith, 'Chemical heat pumping and energy storage', in D. Gray (ed.), *Proceedings of the Heat Pump Workshop held at the Cosener's House, Abingdon, 26–27 September 1977,* Rutherford Laboratory Report RL–77–145/C).

33

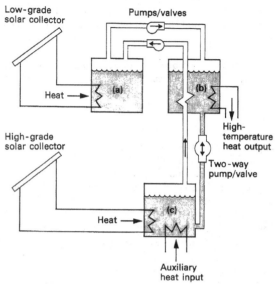

Figure 10 A chemical heat pump system. This is in principle a chemically closed system. (After P. F. Smith, 'Chemical heat pumping and energy storage'.)

absorption reservoir can be passed periodically. This storage reservoir is brought to a still higher temperature by a high-temperature solar collector or, if necessary, by an auxiliary heat source which could be electrical. It serves to drive off water vapour from the acid solution and back into the water reservoir, picking up heat from the absorption reservoir on the way. This reconcentrates the acid in the storage reservoir, whence it can be passed back into the vapour absorption reservoir. It is from the vapour absorption reservoir that useful output heat can be drawn, at temperatures typically 60–100 C for input temperatures below 20 C.

Not only sulphuric acid and water but a large number of other chemical combinations have been considered for such heat pumps, such as sodium hydroxide and water, water and ammonia, or glycerol and methanol. Their commercial viability has yet to be demonstrated.

chlorophyll A complex organic substance (a magnesium porphyrin) which is present in all green plants and is active in the process of **photosynthesis**, by which sunlight is used by the plant. It makes it possible for water and carbon dioxide to be brought together to produce carbohydrates, oxygen being given off as a by-product.

CHP (combined heat and power)   The idea that electricity generation should be combined with processes which would make use of the otherwise wasted low-grade heat. Electricity can then be produced alongside, say, domestic hot water, with an overall efficiency perhaps twice that of plant generating electricity alone.

Ci   See **curie**.

climate   The conditions pertaining in any particular region which determine the patterns of local weather and vegetation. While weather changes from day to day, climate changes only over long spans of time.

In recent years it has been realised that man-made changes in climate are now at least as important as purely natural changes. One example is the disruption of the natural **carbon dioxide** cycle; another is the effect of agriculture over the centuries on **albedo** and rainfall patterns. To some extent these anthropogenic effects may cancel one another out, but the present level of our knowledge is not such that the future climate can be predicted with confidence.

Clinch River   Site near Oak Ridge, Tennessee, USA, proposed for a demonstration fast breeder reactor.

coal   Any solid fossil hydrocarbon fuel. There are many types of coal, ranging from almost pure hydrocarbon with very few impurities down to brown coal or lignite which contains also compounds of oxygen, nitrogen, etc. See also **fossil fuels, fuel**.

coal liquefaction   The name of a range of methods by which a liquid fuel may be produced from coal. In the past this has been done on a large scale in Germany and in South Africa by an indirect method (the Fischer-Tropsch method) in which the coal is first used to give gas (a mixture of hydrogen and carbon monoxide) which is then reduced catalytically to a liquid hydrocarbon fuel. If the liquid fuel is the only output from such a plant, the process is no more than about 40 per cent efficient.

More advanced methods of direct coal liquefaction exist: the pyrolysis of coal giving vapours which condense into fuel oils, and the solvent extraction method by which crushed coal is slurried in oil and passed over a hot catalytic reactor. In ways like these efficiencies of up to 70 per cent are achievable, and perhaps more if the liquefaction plant forms part of a larger complex in which the non-liquefied hydrocarbons are made use of. See also **coalplex**.

coalplex   A proposed type of industrial complex in which coal would be used as input to give a range of secondary fuels (graded coal, liquid fuel, SNG, electricity, and perhaps hot water for district heating) and chemical products. Such a system could achieve a much higher efficiency than any plant devoted to a single coal product.

coefficient of performance   A measure of the effectiveness of a heat pump.

cogeneration   Another term for **CHP**.

coke   The solid fuel produced by the heat-treatment of coal. It contains about 80 per cent carbon and has a calorific value of 28 MJ/kg. Coke is a by-product of gas production from coal, and (nowadays more often) is manufactured for its own sake as an ideal fuel for the smelting and reduction of metals, especially steel. See also **fuel**.

combined heat and power   See **CHP**.

compressed air   A medium which has been proposed for the storage of energy. When air (or any other gas) is compressed to a pressure P, it is thereby given an energy density of, very approximately,

$$P \cdot \ln(P/P_a)$$

where P_a is the atmospheric pressure. If the pressures are expressed in pascals, the energy density from the above formula will be in joules per cubic metre.

Large-scale compressed air energy storage can take place in pressure tanks, depleted oilfields, subterranean caverns created by nuclear explosions, and in many other kinds of container. Like pumped hydroelectric storage, it can be effective for giving electricity to follow rapidly varying demand, with the input compression power being supplied by nuclear electricity, tidal energy or the like.

Compressed air can yield up its energy into the form of electricity either through a straightforward expansion turbine generator or through being linked to a fuel-burning turbine. Complex integrated systems can be designed in which compressed air storage leads to high system efficiency at modest cost: Figure 11 shows an example.

conduction   (1) The flow of electricity through solid conductors (wires), ionised liquids (electrolytes) or ionised gases (plasmas).

(2) The diffusion of heat through a material due to the transfer of energy between colliding molecules; it is distinct from **convection**.

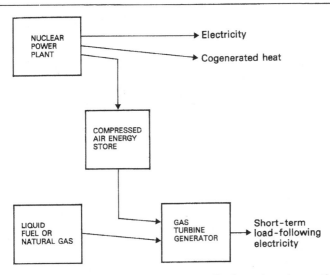

Figure 11 Compressed air energy storage. In the system shown, the use of such a store permits high overall efficiency to be achieved.

conductivity   The rate at which heat will diffuse through a substance in response to a temperature gradient. Since the heat flow rate would be in watts per square metre, and the temperature gradient in Kelvins per metre, the conductivity is measured in watts per metre per Kelvin. The values for some common substances are given in Table 3.

Table 3 *Heat conductivities*

Substance	Conductivity (W/m/K)	Substance	Conductivity (W/m/K)
Air	0.026	Cork	*ca.* 0.05
CO_2	0.017	Glass	1.0
Helium	0.15	Ice	1.7
Hydrogen	0.18	Iron	84.0
Krypton	0.010	Lead	35.0
Xenon	0.006	Mineral wool	0.04
		Polystyrene foam	0.03
Water	0.60	Polyurethane foam	0.02
		Silicon	170.0
Aluminium	235.0	Snow	0.16
Asbestos	0.1	Stainless steel	14.0
Cement mortar	0.6	Wood	*ca.* 0.1
Concrete	0.8		

This is distinct from electrical conductivity, which is a measure of how readily electricity will pass through an electrically conducting material.

conservation of energy The physical principle that energy cannot be annihilated or created out of nothing; it can be converted only from one form into another. See **Noether's Theorem** and **energy**. The principle of the conservation of energy has nothing to do with **energy conservation**.

control rod In a nuclear fission reactor, neutron-absorbing control rods made from boron or cadmium compounds are inserted or withdrawn from the reactor core to control it.

convection A way in which heat flows through a volume of gas or liquid. Heating brings about expansion, and therefore a lowering of density, with the result that a hotter part of a fluid will become more buoyant than the rest and will rise up. Convection currents in air are an important consideration in domestic energy systems: they can lead to waste, for example when warm air collects uselessly at the top of a high-ceilinged room; or convection can be used to good effect as in the **Trombe wall**.

conversions See 'Units'.

cooling pond A water-filled tank in which high-level nuclear waste, such as used fuel, can be stored while its radioactive heat production delays permanent disposal or reprocessing. In the cooling pond water convection will keep the material at a reasonable temperature until the radioactivity has largely died away; this may take several months or a few years.

core In a nuclear reactor, the core is the central part where the energy-producing **fission** or **fusion** actually occurs. See also **nuclear reactors**.

cracking The breaking down of heavy hydrocarbon molecules to smaller, more volatile, molecules.

critical mass The mass of a fissile material which, when compacted together, would be sufficient to sustain a **chain reaction**. The value of the critical mass depends on the type of the material and its degree of enrichment.

crude oil   Liquid fossil hydrocarbon in the form in which it is extracted from the ground. See also **oil, fossil fuels, fuel.**

cryogenics   The technology of very low temperatures, i.e. temperatures below, say, 10 or 20 K, more than 250 centigrade degrees below freezing point. At such temperatures many metals become superconducting and so may pass large currents without consuming much electrical power. This has potential applications in long-distance electricity distribution and in the production of high magnetic fields, for example in magnetic confinement **fusion reactors.**

curie (Ci)   The unit of radioactivity of any sample of material; it is defined as being equal to 3.7×10^{10} disintegrations per second, corresponding almost to the radioactivity of 1 gram of the radium isotope ^{226}Ra.

For any radioactive substance, the activity is given by

$$\text{Activity (Ci)} = 1.13 \times 10^{16} \times M/(A \cdot t_{1/2})$$

where M is the mass of the sample in kilograms, A is the mass number (i.e. 226 for ^{226}Ra, 239 for ^{239}Pu, etc.) and $t_{1/2}$ is the substance's half-life in seconds.

An alternative measure of radioactivity is the SI unit, the **becquerel.** 1 Ci = 37 GBq.

curium   The element of atomic number $Z = 96$, one of the actinide metals. Its most stable isotope is ^{247}Cm which has a half-life of 16 million years, but the most useful isotope has turned out to be ^{244}Cm, which has a half-life of 18 years and by its decay provides heat at the rate of 2.9 kW kg^{-1}. This heat energy has been used in generators of electricity for satellites in which an internal, long-term, energy supply is needed.

CV (abbr. for cheval vapeur)   The metric counterpart of 'horsepower', equal to 0.986 hp or 0.735 kW.

Daniell cell   A kind of electrical **storage cell** of which the anode is of copper and the cathode of zinc; the electrolyte between them is dilute sulphuric acid.

Darrieus   The name given to a type of vertical-axis wind-energy machine with thin, aerofoil-like vanes. See Figure 50 under **wind energy**.

DC   See **direct current**.

deep mining   Coal-mining below a depth of about 1,000 m. Mines exist today which extend well below 1,300 m.

deforestation   The process by which mankind's activities are reducing the earth's natural covering of forests. Deforestation is leading to a serious shift in the global **carbon cycle**, but is proceeding rapidly under the pressure of demand for fresh agricultural land and, in some countries, the demand for firewood. In a historical context, one can see how deforestation began around the Mediterranean in Classical times, spread elsewhere in Europe and Asia subsequently, and followed the European empires to Africa, India and other parts of the world. Deforestation has proceeded steadily, hand-in-hand with man's physical mastery of the earth, and it can now be foreseen that within a few decades the only remaining areas of extensive natural forest will be the boreal forests of northern Canada and Siberia and a proportion of the Amazon Basin's tropical rain forest.

degree   The unit of **temperature** (or of temperature difference) which for the Kelvin and Celsius scales is roughly equal to 1 per cent of the temperature difference between melting ice and boiling water. The Fahrenheit degree is smaller by a factor of five-ninths.

More precisely, the degree is defined as equal to one part in 273.16 of the absolute temperature at the 'triple point' of water having the isotopic composition of seawater.

degree day   To estimate the energy needed to heat a building to a comfortable temperature, one needs information about the average outside ambient temperature, and this information is provided in a convenient form by 'degree days'.

The number of degree days in a period of time is got by adding, day by day, the 24-hour averages of the amounts by which the outside temperatures fall below a certain base temperature: any excess of the outside temperature over the base value is not taken into the average. The base temperature is generally taken to be 15.5 C (60 F), since it has been found that when the outside temperature reaches that value it is not necessary to heat buildings; incidental heat gain (e.g. from lighting) will then keep the inside temperature at a comfortable level of about 18.5 C (65 F).

Whatever the method of heating a building, the cost is in proportion to the number of degree days experienced, and the degree days per month in different regions are published both (a) in the form of long-term averages so that energy use estimates may be made, and (b) as actual figures for particular years so that fuel use efficiency may be monitored.

As an example: in south-eastern England, in December, a twenty-year average gives 358 degree days (Celsius) to be expected over the 31 days, but in 1977 only 291 were actually experienced, so heating bills should have been 19 per cent lower than usual for that month.

delayed neutron   In the core of a nuclear fission reactor, neutrons are produced out of the fissile nuclei directly at the moment of fission ('prompt' neutrons) and also indirectly through intermediate fission products which are short lived and give rise to neutrons when they decay. The latter, termed 'delayed neutrons', carry a time delay of a second or two in the chain reaction loop and so are vital in permitting the nuclear reaction to be safely controlled and harnessed.

Department of Energy   (1) In the USA, the Department of Energy was created in 1977 out of the previous Energy Research and Development Administration (ERDA); ERDA had itself been formed in 1975 from sections of the **Atomic Energy Commission** (AEC) and other agencies.

(2) In the UK, the Department of Energy is the government ministry with overall responsibility for energy affairs.

depleted uranium   Uranium which differs from natural uranium by having had some of the fissile isotope, ^{235}U, removed. It is a by-product of enrichment processes which give uranium enhanced in ^{235}U. Depleted uranium consists of little else but the heavier isotope, ^{238}U, and it has certain specialised applications such as for calorimetry in high-energy particle physics and for making armour-piercing shells.

derv (abbr. for diesel engine road vehicle)   A term used in the UK for the fuel for fast-running diesel engines.

desalination   The production of pure water from salty or brackish water. Desalination is important for the supply of drinking water or irrigation water in many parts of the world. Desalination on a large scale requires a high energy input, and combined systems have been built using nuclear power to give electricity and also to desalinate sea water. On a small scale, solar energy can readily be used in a

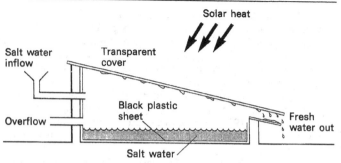

Figure 12 A solar still.

'solar still' (see Figure 12): solar radiation passes through the transparent plastic cover and is then absorbed by the salt water inside or by the black lining. There is a rise in temperature and humidity within the container, and vapour is driven off from the salt water to condense on the underside of the cover.

deuterium   A form of hydrogen, having for its atomic nucleus a proton combined with a neutron rather than a proton alone. It is sometimes called 'heavy hydrogen', and occurs naturally mixed in ordinary hydrogen at a concentration of about 300 parts per million by weight. Deuterium has its own symbol, D, although it is an isotope of hydrogen and so is sometimes referred to as ^{2}H. Its nucleus is the 'deuteron'.

As a fuel for nuclear fusion, deuterium has been used in nuclear weapons and may in the future have a role in the controlled generation of energy. It is crucial to the production of energy within the sun. In some nuclear fission reactors (notably the Canadian deuterium-uranium reactor, **CANDU**) it has been used in the form of heavy water, D_2O, as a coolant and moderator.

diesel   The name given to internal combustion engines in which the compression of the fuel/air mixture is sufficient to ignite it, in contrast to most automobile engines which have a smaller compression ratio and use spark plugs for ignition. Diesel engines, while generally heavier and more expensive than spark ignition engines, have the advantages of better fuel economy, good cold-starting, a longer lifetime and generally less harmful exhaust emissions.

diesel cycle   A **thermodynamic cycle** which is the basis of the diesel engine. The cycle, illustrated in Figure 13 in terms of pressure and volume, consists of (1) the isentropic compression of an air-fuel mixture, causing it to warm up until (2) there is combustion, heat energy being produced at constant pressure, then (3) mechanical power is given out through the isentropic expansion of the gas, and finally (4) at fixed volume, the warm exhaust gas is replaced by fresh air and fuel at atmospheric pressure. The theoretical efficiency of the cycle depends in a complicated way on the compression ratio V_a/V_b and on the ratio of volumes before and after ignition, V_c/V_b. Ideally, one should have a high compression ratio and a low ignition ratio.

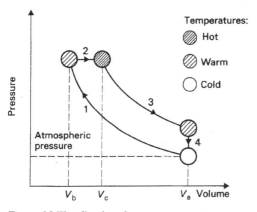

Figure 13 The diesel cycle.

It must be stressed that the diesel cycle is an idealisation of what goes on in an actual diesel engine (see **diesel**).

digester   A container in which biological material is fermented so as to give off methane or alcohol which can be used as a fuel. See also **biological energy**.

direct current (DC)   An electric current in which the flow of electrons is in a constant direction (unlike alternating current). Direct current is given by storage cells and is needed for certain purposes such as electrolysis, but it is disadvantageous when high voltages are being handled and so alternating currents are much more common in the electricity supply industry. See also **electricity**.

district heating   The use of piped hot water to provide heating for homes over a wide area, e.g. for a number of neighbouring small towns. District heating is feasible as a form of 'combined heat and power' (**CHP**) or **cogeneration** whereby a power station gives useful hot water as well as electricity, the overall efficiency being much higher than that for an all-electric system.

domestic energy Energy used in the home, mainly for heating, cooling, lighting and cooking: domestic energy accounts for something like 40 per cent of energy consumption in developed Western countries. There is recognised to be wide scope for the more effective use of energy in homes through conservation measures, modern machinery and materials, and 'alternative' energy sources. In fact, it is now technically and economically feasible to construct houses which will be virtually autonomous in energy terms, deriving power mainly from the sun and wind and needing an external supply of commercial energy only as a back-up against periods of exceptional need.

Ideally, a domestic energy system is an integrated set of several components, some active and some passive. Passive components include windows, high-heat-capacity walls (such as the **Trombe wall**), wind screens, wall coatings chosen for their radiation properties, and heat storage media. Active components include stoves, boilers, heat pumps, heat exchangers, windmills, electric heaters and motors, and associated electronic control equipment. However, it must be emphasised that although a new dwelling may be profitably equipped in this sort of way, the situation is quite different for older existing buildings. 'Retrofitting' existing buildings with new energy systems is often 'on the edge' economically, but it has to be seriously considered because of the enormous numbers of energy-inefficient older buildings which still have a long life ahead of them. This problem, which is as much economic and social as technical, is perhaps the main challenge in the domestic energy field.

double glazing The use of two parallel sheets of glass instead of one to cut down heat loss through windows. In principle double glazing can drastically reduce conductive heat loss, since the air between the two panes is more or less static and has a conductivity much lower than a solid material such as glass itself. See also **windows, domestic energy**.

Dounreay The site in Caithness, Scotland, of the UK's prototype **fast breeder** nuclear fission reactor.

dynamo A contraction of 'dynamo-electric machine', a term occasionally used for a generator of electricity from mechanical power. See also **generator**.

earth   The planet which mankind inhabits is one of nine which, together with the sun itself and numerous minor bodies, forms the solar system. The earth is probably the only planet in the system ever to have given rise to life, since reasonable climatic conditions would not occur for a planet much further from or nearer to the sun.

Radiant **solar energy** reaches the earth at a rate of some 0.173 exawatts, and since the average albedo is 30 per cent, about 50 petawatts are immediately reflected back into space. The solar radiation which is absorbed (say, 0.12 exawatts) is balanced by the radiation from the earth, radiation which is at invisible infra-red wavelengths because of the low temperature of the earth compared with the sun. In the inner-space environment in the vicinity of the earth, the earth's infra-red radiation is 17 per cent as intense in energy terms as the sun's light.

In comparison with radiation, the earth's other energy flows are for most purposes negligible. **Geothermal energy** is a geologically vital power source, but has been exploited commercially only in a few favoured locations. The same is true of the tides, by which gravitational and rotational energy are dissipated.

ECCS   See **emergency core-cooling system**.

efficiency   For any kind of energy conversion system the efficiency is the ratio of the useful energy output to the energy input which could potentially be used. For example, the efficiency of photosynthesis is no more than about 2 per cent, but photovoltaic electricity can be produced from sunlight with an efficiency approaching 20 per cent.

einsteinium (symbol Es)   The element of atomic number $Z = 99$, one of the **actinide** metals. Einsteinium occurs only when made artificially and none of its isotopes has a half-life greater than 1 year.

Einstein's equation   The equation $E = mc^2$, expressing the equivalence of mass to energy at an 'exchange rate' of 89.9 PJ/kg. An everyday quantity of energy will correspond to an unmeasurably small amount of mass: for example, when half a gallon of petroleum is burned there is heat released with a net loss in mass of about one-millionth of a gram.

electric car   A vehicle driven by an electric motor with energy obtained, usually, from a storage cell or fuel cell.

electric motor   A device for transforming electrical energy into a mechanical form. Electric motors usually work by letting the electric current flow around a coil within a magnetic field provided by an iron magnet; a rotatory force on the coil results, which can easily be used to perform work such as the driving of a pump. Electric motors can be designed to work from DC or AC electricity, and very high efficiencies can in principle be achieved.

It has been pointed out recently that a high proportion of electricity consumption goes to run motors which are very much less efficient than they could be, either because they are running at a power above or below their optimum, or because the alternating current is badly 'trimmed' in waveform and phase within the motor, or for other reasons. Such problems can be cured economically by using modern electronics to the full, and substantial savings are likely to be achieved in this way over the next few years.

electricity   May be thought of as a convenient way of transmitting energy from place to place and then allowing it to be converted at high efficiency into mechanical power, heat or other forms. However, most electricity is generated in a relatively inefficient way from heat got from the combustion of fossil fuels: for thermodynamical reasons this type of 'thermal' electricity generation is rarely achieved with an efficiency more than about 40 per cent. Another category of sources is 'primary' electricity, which includes nuclear, hydro and the like.

Table 4 *Central electricity generation: capacity and production (1978)*

Type	Power installed (GW)	% use	Energy produced (EJ)
Thermal	1,180	53	19.9
Hydro	387	46	5.6
Nuclear	106	57	1.9
All types	1,673	52	27.4

Table 4 shows the installed power capacity and production of electricity worldwide. Total electricity consumption is equivalent to almost 10 per cent of gross world primary energy, but because of the inefficiency mentioned above over 25 per cent of primary energy is being devoted to electricity production.

electrode A terminal linking conducting wires from an electrical circuit with a poorly-conducting medium such as the electrolyte within a storage cell. According to the direction of flow of the current, it may be necessary to distinguish between a positive electrode, or **anode**, and a negative electrode, or cathode.

electrolysis The decomposition of a chemical substance by the passing of electricity through it. In most applications the substance is dissolved in a liquid and the products of the decomposition are actually given off at electrodes immersed in the liquid which lead the electric current in and out. A particularly interesting case is the electrolysis of water itself into hydrogen and oxygen: this is a way of producing a fuel, hydrogen, from electrical energy which could not be easily stored in any other way.

electromagnetic radiation A general term for radio waves, microwaves, infra-red waves, visible light, ultra-violet waves, X-rays and gamma-rays, all of which are similar in nature and can be regarded as due to interplaying electric and magnetic fields. Electromagnetic radiation propagates through space at a universal speed of 0.3 gigametres per second in 'packets' or quanta ('photons'), with energy in proportion to the frequency of the waves. See also **Planck's constant**.

electromagnetism The phenomena of electricity and magnetism and their effects on matter.

A key concept is that of electric and magnetic fields, whose deep inter-relationship is illustrated by the fact that a varying electric field will induce a magnetic field, while a varying magnetic field will induce an electric field. Their essential unity is reflected in the term 'electromagnetism'. Some of the fundamental particles of which matter is composed are acted on by forces in the presence of electromagnetic fields; such particles are said to be 'charged', and one of the most important of them in practice is the **electron**. All chemical reactions arise from electromagnetic forces involving electrons.

Electromagnetic fields carry energy, and the energy density (in the absence of matter) is given by

$$U = \tfrac{1}{2} \cdot (\epsilon_o E^2 + \mu_o H^2)$$

Here, U is in joules per cubic metre, E is the electric field in volts per metre and H is the magnetic field in amperes per metre. ϵ_o and μ_o are constants equal to 8.84×10^{-12} and 1.26×10^{-6} respectively. It is no accident that $(\epsilon_o \cdot \mu_o)^{-\frac{1}{2}}$ is equal to the velocity of light.

electromotive force (emf) An old term for electrical potential or voltage. See also **volt, electricity.**

electron A type of fundamental particle, extremely tiny and light even by the standards of atomic and nuclear physics. It weighs 9.1×10^{-31} kg, and carries an electric charge of 1.6×10^{-19} coulombs. By convention, this charge is negative in sign, while the **proton** has a balancing positive charge. In ordinary matter electrons are bound by electrical attraction close to the proton-containing nuclei of atoms.

Electricity in everyday life arises from a flow of electrons through matter, and especially through metals; metallic atoms contain mobile 'conduction' electrons which permit an easy flow.

Energetic electrons, not bound to atoms, are produced in radioactive decay processes, and are then often known as 'beta-particles'. Beta-decay may also produce positively charged electrons, otherwise called positrons, which are the antiparticles of normal electrons.

electron volt A unit of energy (abbr. eV) equal to the energy transferred when an electron, or any particle having the same charge as an electron, moves through an electric potential difference of one volt. Because the charge of the electron is 1.6×10^{-19} coulombs, an electron volt is equal to 1.6×10^{-19} joules. See also 'Units'.

element A kind of atom having particular chemical properties characterised by the **atomic number.** Over 100 different elements exist, ranging from hydrogen (atomic number $Z = 1$) up to laurencium ($Z = 103$) and beyond.

emergency core-cooling system (ECCS) In a nuclear fission reactor, this is a system to provide a flow of cooling water separate from the coolant circuit normally used to transfer heat energy out of the reactor core. The ECCS is intended to be available whenever, for whatever reason, the reactor's normal cooling system fails to operate adequately.

emissivity (SI symbol ϵ) is a measure of how effectively a surface will radiate away heat or light. It is properly defined as the ratio between the power radiated by the surface per unit area and that which would be radiated by an ideal 'black body' at the same temperature.

By consideration of the conditions for thermal equilibrium, it can be shown that the emissivity of a surface is equal to its **absorptivity** for radiation of the same temperature. The difference between emissivity and absorptivity is that the former depends on the wavelengths emitted (and therefore on the temperature of the body itself) whereas absorptivity depends on the wavelengths incident (and so on the temperature of the sun or other illuminator).

To avoid confusion, the convention is recommended whereby 'absorptivity' is used to refer to visible light, while the word 'emissivity' is used for infra-red radiation such as is given off by everyday objects. Values for these quantities are given in Table 5 for a few commonplace materials.

Table 5 *Emissivities or absorptivities (%)**

Surface	Absorptivity α (visible light, *ca*. 6,000 K)	Emissivity ϵ (radiant heat, *ca*. 300 K)
Aluminium (oxidised)	30	25
Aluminium (polished)	20	5
Black paint	90	80
Copper (oxidised)	70	40
Copper (polished)	40	2.5
Glass	(transparent)	94
Mirror	5	80
Newspaper	40	92
Snow	7	97
Water	(transparent)	94
White paint	20	85

*All these values are approximate and for guidance only: in practice wide variations occur; e.g. between different types of paint.

Note that the α/ϵ ratio is important in determining the equilibrium temperature of any object in sunlight. See also **Stefan–Boltzmann law, reflectivity.**

endothermic   An endothermic reaction or process is one in which energy is absorbed, i.e. is converted into a latent form. In particular, endothermic chemical reactions involve the absorption of heat into a form of chemical energy. In contrast, **exothermic** reactions give off heat.

energy   The physical quantity which can manifest itself as heat, as mechanical work, as motion, and in the binding of matter by nuclear or chemical forces. The modern concept of energy was developed early this century following the work of Einstein, whose special theory of relativity made it clear that mass itself is a manifestation of energy, and the pioneers of quantum mechanics, which led to a vastly improved understanding of energy transfer at the microscopic level.

Although the concept of energy is now unified, and we understand it to be indestructible and uncreatable, nevertheless the differences between the various forms of energy are of paramount practical importance. These differences are reflected in the range of ways in which energy is commonly measured (see Table 6, also 'Units', **joule**).

Table 6 *Energy magnitudes*

Form	Energy (J)
The Big Bang	10^{68}
Supernova	10^{43}
Sun's annual radiation	10^{34}
Fusion of ocean's hydrogen	10^{34}
Earth's internal heat	10^{31}
Earth's spin	10^{29}
Fission of ocean's uranium	10^{26}
Sun's annual radiation to earth	10^{25}
Total fossil fuel resources	10^{23}
Annual marine biomass growth	10^{21}
Volcanic eruption	10^{19}
Annual exploitable tidal energy	10^{18}
Very big H-bomb	10^{17}
Kilogram of ^{235}U	10^{14}
Lightning flash	10^{10}
Annual human diet	10^{9}
One hamburger	10^{6}
Motion of a car	10^{5}
Melting of an ice cube	10^{4}
Coin falling to the ground	10^{-1}
Fission of single uranium nucleus	10^{-11}
One quantum of visible light	10^{-19}

Energy is closely related to **force**; when a force causes an object to move, energy is being transferred from the force-field into the form of the object's kinetic energy. At root, there are in nature only two or three different kinds of force, namely (a) the gravitational force which holds the earth together and is responsible for the energy yielded up by falling objects, (b) the 'electroweak' forces which include those of electricity and magnetism and also weak nuclear forces involving particles like the electron, and (c) the strong nuclear forces, best explained in terms of the 'chromodynamic' forces between quarks. Seventy-five years after Einstein's seminal work, the subject remains as progressive and lively as ever.

energy analysis   A study of all the energy flows necessary for carrying out some process or project, to establish whether or not the process is worth while from the point of view of energy economy.

To give a very simple example: electric motors are much more efficient than combustion engines, and so it might seem that electric cars should be more efficient than conventional ones. However, a complete energy analysis must take into account the provision of electricity for recharging the electric car's batteries, and heat losses in the central generation of that electricity from, say, coal. One then finds that electric cars offer no great overall saving of energy.

energy audit   By analogy with a financial audit, an energy audit is an examination of all the energy use of an establishment (which might be a hospital, a block of offices, a private home, an industrial plant, etc.) to determine what the energy is actually used for and where it ultimately goes. An energy audit is an essential first step before informed decisions can be made on fuel purchasing policy, conservation measures, etc.

energy conservation   Not to be confused with the **conservation of energy**, which is a law of nature, energy conservation is the careful and sparing use of energy with a view to conserving the natural resources from which energy is derived (especially fossil hydrocarbons) and minimising environmental pollution. By implementing a range of quite simple technical 'fixes', the energy consumption of most developed nations could be reduced perhaps by as much as 50 per cent, and even in purely financial terms energy conservation has been recognised as a better medium-term investment than additional energy supply capacity.

energy intensity   The amount of energy which must be used to yield a certain quantity (a kilogram, or a tonne, or a dollar's worth) of any particular product.

energy management   The task of controlling efficiently the use of energy by an establishment or organisation. Energy management requires the establishment of an energy audit, the implementation of conservation procedures as appropriate, the selection and purchase of fuels, and defining a strategy for the replacement of energy-wasteful capital plant in the long term.

energy storage Many natural sources of energy such as the wind and the tides supply power not when it is needed by consumers but at other, uncontrollable, times. Even artificial energy sources, such as nuclear reactors, are often unable to give energy exactly when it is needed because it is technically difficult (and expensive) to vary the energy output to match the fluctuating pattern of demand. For these reasons energy storage systems are of great importance and on the large scale 'pumped hydroelectric' schemes are being increasingly used for this purpose. On the small scale, heat storage devices and electric storage cells are valuable. Furthermore, certain secondary fuels such as hydrogen can be regarded as media for energy storage and may become widely used for that purpose in the future.

energy vector A medium for the transfer of energy from one place to another. Electricity, refined liquid fuel, liquefied natural gas, coal slurry and piped hot water are just a few of the many energy vectors in use.

enriched uranium Natural uranium consists almost entirely of the isotope ^{238}U, with just 0.7 per cent being of the lighter, fissile, isotope ^{235}U. Enriched uranium has a proportion of ^{235}U higher than that.

enrichment The proportion of ^{235}U in a sample of enriched uranium. Most commercial reactors use uranium with an enrichment of the order of 2 or 3 per cent; but for military purposes much higher enrichments, between 50 and 100 per cent, are sometimes used.

enthalpy Because of the energy transferred in the expansion or compression of a gas, it can be convenient to define the quantity 'enthalpy', H, by

$$H = U + p \cdot V$$

where p and V are the pressure and volume of a quantity of gas and U is its internal energy.

entropy A thermodynamic variable, usually denoted by S, which can be defined for any system and is measured in units of joules per kelvin. As the system evolves, the entropy change dS is given by

$$dS \geqslant \Sigma \, (dQ/T)$$

where the summation is over the parts of the system, dQ being the heat flows into the different parts and T the temperatures. The equality holds for thermodynamically reversible change, but in general the entropy change dS is greater; for an isolated system dS is always greater than zero.

environment The surroundings—physical, biological and social—in which mankind lives. The word is sometimes applied broadly to the whole of the earth's biosphere, and sometimes much more narrowly to small geographical areas or even to individual buildings or rooms. The interdependence of parts of the environment, the sensitivity of its balance, and our ignorance of exactly how the environment works, together make it important to assess carefully the likely impact of major energy developments. An 'environmental impact statement' is now considered an essential part of any large-scale proposal.

erg A unit of energy now largely superseded, equal to 10^{-7} J. See also 'Units'.

ethane (C_2H_6) A light hydrocarbon gas, one of the alkanes with a calorific value of 48 MJ/kg.

ethanol (CH_3CH_2OH) The modern name for ethyl alcohol, which is usable as a fuel and has a calorific value of 28 MJ/kg. See also **alcohol, biological energy**.

ethene (or ethylene) An alkene hydrocarbon gas, chemical formula C_2H_4, with a calorific value of 47 MJ/kg.

exothermic An exothermic reaction is one which gives off energy, usually in the form of heat. Combustible fuels burn exothermically, the amount of heat being given by the calorific value of each fuel.

exponential Exponentials are most familiar in the context of quantities increasing or decreasing with time. As an example, consider a country whose annual energy consumption C is doubling every ten years:

$$C = C_o \cdot 2^{(t - t_o)/10}$$

Here, 2 is raised to a 'power', or 'exponent', which is the number of decades at time t since an earlier time t_o at which the energy consumption was equal to C_o. That formula can be written in the different form

$$C = C_o \cdot e^{\alpha (t - t_o)}$$

where e is the number 2.7183 (chosen as a convention because it has convenient mathematical properties) and α is in this case 0.0693. Another way of writing the same thing is

$$C = C_0 \cdot \exp(\alpha(t - t_0))$$

where 'exp' is the standard abbreviation for 'exponential'. The value of α tells us that C is increasing at an annual rate of 6.93 per cent. This sort of growth, where the quantity's *rate* of growth is a proportion of the *amount* at each instant, is 'exponential'.

A useful rule of thumb true for modest growth rates is:

$$\text{doubling time} = \frac{70}{\text{annual } \% \text{ increase}}$$

Radioactive decay provides an example of a 'negative exponential', i.e. a quantity falling each year by a fixed proportion of itself. A quantity of a radioactive substance will decay like

$$Q = Q_0 \cdot e^{-\alpha(t - t_0)}$$

where Q_0 is the quantity at time t_0 and Q is that at any subsequent time t. In the case of, say, plutonium (^{239}Pu), the coefficient α is 28.4×10^{-6} if t is in units of years. The inverse of α, i.e. 35,202, is the 'mean life' of plutonium in years; the 'half-life' is $\ln2/\alpha$ or 24,400 years.

external combustion engine   An internal combustion engine is driven by hot gas which is directly produced by the combustion of a fuel within the engine. In the external combustion engine the fuel is kept quite separate from the gas which it heats: the steam engine is the most familiar example.

A form of external combustion engine in which there is much current interest is the **Stirling engine**.

Fahrenheit   The name of a scale of **temperature** in which the melting point of ice is taken to be at 32 degrees and the boiling point of water 180 degrees higher. With the widespread modern standardisation to the Kelvin and Celsius scales, the Fahrenheit scale is now falling into disuse.

fallout   Radioactive material in the form of dust or gas, released into the air on being produced by a nuclear explosion or other incident.

fast breeder   A nuclear fission reactor in the core of which fast neutrons are present so as to yield a substantial amount of plutonium through the absorption of fast neutrons by the uranium isotope ^{238}U. See also **nuclear reactors, breeder**.

fast neutrons   Those neutrons with kinetic energy in the range 0.1 to 10 MeV, i.e. such as are given off in nuclear fission. See also **nuclear reactors**.

FBR   Abbr. for **fast breeder** reactor.

fermium   The element of atomic number $Z = 100$ (symbol Fm), one of the **actinide** metals.

fertile   In the context of nuclear energy, a fertile nucleus is one which can be converted into a fissile one through absorbing a neutron. See also **breeder**.

firewood   See **wood**.

first law   The first law of **thermodynamics**, which is that energy is a conserved quantity which can change its form but can never be created or destroyed.

fissile   A type of nucleus which will readily undergo fission upon absorbing a neutron. The fissile nuclei important in practice are isotopes of uranium (^{233}U and ^{235}U) and of plutonium (especially ^{239}Pu). See also **nuclear reactors**.

fission   The splitting of a heavy nucleus into two smaller nuclei, generally accompanied by other fragments such as neutrons and gamma-rays and with energy amounting to about 200 MeV (32 pJ) appearing as heat. Fission is occasionally spontaneous but can be induced in fissile nuclei by neutrons; this is the principle of the chain reaction on which nuclear fission power in practice is based.

flaring   The burning-off of natural gas found in conjunction with oil in oilfields. With the value of natural gas now widely appreciated flaring is becoming uncommon.

flash distillation   A method of distilling water in large quantities, applied in particular to the desalination of seawater. The water is

55

heated to a temperature of the order of 100 C, or a little more, but kept under sufficient pressure to stop it boiling. It is then fed through a succession of chambers, each at a lower pressure than the previous one, and at each stage there is a rapid evaporation ('flash') giving vapour. The vapour is condensed on condensers cooled by the incoming seawater (see Figure 14), giving pure water.

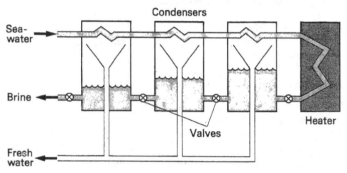

Figure 14 A flash distillation system for seawater desalination driven by a source of medium-grade (80–100 C) heat.

flat-plate collector or 'solar panel'   A rectangular panel designed to catch the sun's rays without reflecting too much of their energy away again, the trapped heat being transferred to a circulating fluid which can be used in, for example, a heating system. A flat-plate collector may utilise up to about 70 per cent of the solar energy incident on it, but to achieve this efficiency in practice requires careful attention to the siting and orientation of the collector.

fluidised-bed combustion   A finely divided or powdered solid can behave like a fluid when air or any other gas is being blown up through it sufficiently fast. The flowing air supports the weight of each grain of the solid, with the effect that the grains move and mix freely rather than becoming packed together.

This principle is used to bring about the highly efficient combustion of coal of all kinds and other fuels such as that obtained from common refuse. It is the great advantage of many fluidised-bed combustors that they are not fuel-specific, i.e. they can burn high-grade and low-grade fuels with indifference and in some cases can as easily burn fuel oil or gas as well. The principle is illustrated by Figure 15, which shows a steam-raising fluidised-bed combustor burning coal over a current of air.

The fluidised-bed principle can be used to produce fuel gas from

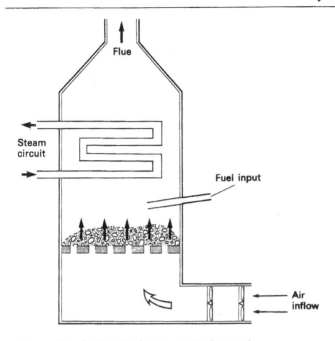

Figure 15 A fluidised-bed steam-raising burner. '

coal in the 'fast fluidised bed' system shown in Figure 16; the coal here is not quite hot enough to burn but is decomposed with the production of carbon monoxide and hydrogen gas. The very speed of the air/gas flow is exploited in a 'cyclone separator' to prevent solid matter from being carried out with the gas. This sort of plant would be integrated with a gas turbine or similar system to consume the gas almost immediately, producing electricity.

fly ash   Particles of ash from the burning of a fuel which are carried along with gaseous combustion products.

flywheel   A wheel which, being heavy and able to spin fast, can be used as a way of storing energy. Flywheels capable of storing several megajoules of energy have been constructed, and the attainable energy density is of the order of 0.2 MJ/kg. Put another way: a flywheel can store as much energy as if it were raised up to a height of 20 km or so.

57

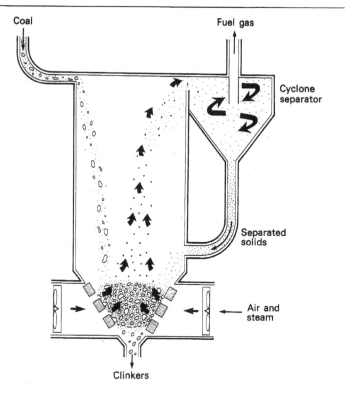

Figure 16 A fluidised bed for the manufacture of coal gas.

force An influence which would cause an object to accelerate. In SI units force is measured in newtons, one newton being that which would make a 1 kg mass accelerate by 1 m per second each second. The movement of a force implies a transfer of energy, and 1 newton moving at 1 metre per second implies 1 joule per second.

fossil fuels Minerals rich in combustible hydrocarbons, the residue of plant material laid down in the distant past. Fossil fuels are usually in solid form (coals) but 10 per cent or so has been in liquid form (crude oil) and almost as much again in gaseous form (natural gas, mostly composed of methane). Besides coal, oil and gas, a good deal of fossil hydrocarbon occurs in intimate mixture with non-combustible material and so is difficult and expensive to extract; oil shales and tar sands are like this.

The energy value of the world's annual fossil fuel consumption is very close to 260 exajoules (see 'Units', also fuel for calorific values, etc.). Of this, 130 EJ is of oil, 80 EJ is of coal, and 50 EJ is of gas. Close to 70 EJ in total are devoted to electricity production, 20 EJ of electricity being thereby generated.

The existing reserves of fossil fuels are known only in very approximate terms. Table 7 shows the amounts which are reasonably well assured and should be economically recoverable. It can be seen that reserves amount to about 500 years' coal supply at the present rate of consumption, and to about 30 years' oil, conclusions which in broad terms are affirmed by an impressive weight of expert opinion. Tar sands add a little to this, and recoverable shale oil may amount to as much again as the existing oil reserves, but it is rather speculative.

Table 7 *Regional distribution of fossil fuel reserves**

	Gas	Oil	Coal
Total reserves (EJ) of which:	2,500	4,000	40,000
America	15%	10%	30%
W. Europe	5%	5%	15%
E. Europe	small	small	5%
Africa	10%	10%	small
USSR	40%	10%	20%
China	small	5%	15%
Rest of Asia	5%	5%	small
Australasia	small	small	5%

*All these figures are uncertain and have been rounded off accordingly.

To the reserves in Table 7 one may add a much larger amount again to allow for hitherto undiscovered or undisclosed fossil fuels which are geologically likely to exist. The ultimate recoverable resources are thus estimated to be 150,000 EJ of coal, 10,000 EJ of oil and 7,000 EJ of natural gas. This is divided regionally in much the same way as the established reserves tabulated, except that the USSR is often considered to have a rather higher proportion of the ultimate coal resources, reaching perhaps 50 per cent of the total.

As far as the future of fossil fuels is concerned, the above remarks are more or less all that can be said with confidence, as intense research in recent years has highlighted gaps in geological knowledge, a paucity of exploration in many parts of the world, and uncertainty about the limits of fuel recovery technology.

freon Any of a range of different halocarbon compounds which are commonly used as the working fluids in heat pumps and refrigerators. For data see **refrigerants**.

fuel Any substance which is a store of energy in that it may be made to react in some way with a release of energy, usually in the form of heat. This reaction may take the form of chemical combustion with oxygen or of a nuclear reaction such as induced fission. The classification of fuels is sketched out in Figure 17. Additionally, electricity is sometimes loosely spoken of as a fuel.

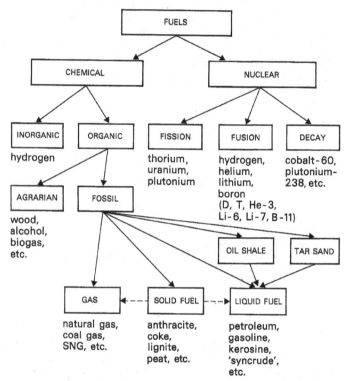

Figure 17 The classification of fuels.

The fuels of greatest practical significance at present are the **fossil fuels** coal, oil and natural gas, all of which are variable mixtures of compounds rich in hydrogen and carbon. Those of highest grade are the 'hydrocarbons' which contain nothing but hydrogen and carbon;

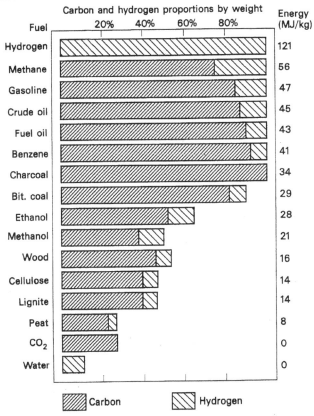

Figure 18 Fuels containing carbon and hydrogen, with approximate calorific values.

others, which are partially oxidised or include other elements, will yield less energy. Figure 18 displays the carbon and hydrogen content of a number of organic fuels and gives their energy content, i.e. calorific value, in megajoules per kilogram (for conversions, see 'Units'). Also included are carbon dioxide and water, the main products of the combustion of the fuels.

Another illustration of the range of organic fuels is Figure 19, with the carbon content of each given against its hydrogen content. Certain categories of fuel (the hydrocarbons, the carbohydrates, the alcohols) lie on straight lines across this plot, and another family of lines defines (approximately) the calorific values.

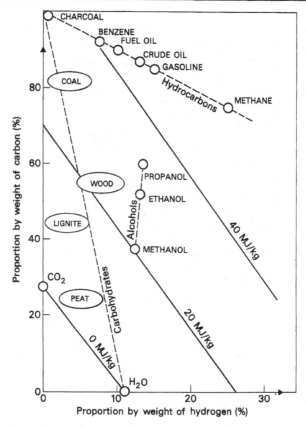

Figure 19 Fuels containing carbon and hydrogen displayed in two dimensions to show their inter-relationships.

fuel cell   An electrical cell which, unlike storage cells, can be continuously fed with a 'fuel' so that the electrical power output is sustained indefinitely. The fuel may be hydrogen or a hydrocarbon, fed into the cell near one of the electrodes; oxygen is fed in at the other. The fuel is consumed electrochemically, producing a voltage but little heat and no atmospheric pollution.

In principle fuel cells, by their direct conversion of chemical energy into electricity, could offer a much higher efficiency than that attainable in conventional fuel-burning plant. Also, fuel cells if perfected would be highly attractive for powering electric-traction vehicles.

fuel cycle   See nuclear fuel cycles.

fuel pellet   In nuclear fusion technology, a small spherical pellet of
between, say, 50 microns and 2 millimetres in diameter. The fuel
contained may be any of several possible mixtures of deuterium,
tritium and other fusion fuels, and there may be discrete layers containing different mixtures.
   Fuel pellets of this kind are being developed for use in inertial
confinement **fusion reactors** driven by laser or heavy ion beams.

fusion   Just as the very heavy elements such as uranium and plutonium can yield energy by being split apart, so the lightest elements
can often be fused together with an energy profit. The reason is
that the elements of intermediate mass are on the whole the most
stable and inert, with comparatively little extractable nuclear energy,
whereas the lightest and heaviest elements are extremes with, so to
speak, energy to spare.
   In nature, the light elements fuse spontaneously under the enormous temperatures and pressures of stellar interiors, releasing the
energy which is the source of the sun's, and other suns', warmth.
To mimic that process artificially, in a controlled way, has seemed
to many to be the ultimate solution to mankind's demand for energy.
It is a goal which seems almost within reach.
   Numerous different fusion reactions have been considered as
candidates for use in a practical fusion reactor, and complex fuel
cycles have been devised around them. Table 8 lists isotopes of the

Table 8 *The light nuclei*

Symbol	Structure (ps, ns)	Mass of nuclide (amu)	Energy potential* TJ/kg
n	(0,1)	1.0087	720
H	(1,0)	1.0078	640
D	(1,1)	2.0141	580
T	(1,2)	3.0160	410
^{3}He	(2,1)	3.0160	410
^{4}He	(2,2)	4.0026	—
^{6}Li	(3,3)	6.0151	160
^{7}Li	(3,4)	7.0160	140
^{9}Be	(4,5)	9.0122	63
^{10}Be	(4,6)	10.0135	63
^{10}B	(5,5)	10.0129	54
^{11}B	(5,6)	11.0093	9

*This is the energy potential with respect to ^{4}He, i.e. the energy which
would be released if fusion reactions occurred with ^{4}He as the only end
product. In practice only a proportion of this potential can be realised.

first five elements (hydrogen, helium, lithium, beryllium and boron) and includes most of those which have been considered as fusion fuels; for completeness the neutron heads the list because of its importance in certain fuel cycles. The table gives the structure of each nuclide (number of protons, number of neutrons) and its mass in the atomic mass units (amus) which are conventional (see 'Units' Table C). The mass in each case is almost equal to the total number of protons and neutrons comprising the nuclide, but exceeds it by a tiny and variable amount which never exceeds 1 per cent of the total. These mass excesses are highly significant, and are the source of fusion energy.

A study of Table 8 will reveal that the helium isotope ^{4}He has, proportionately speaking, the lowest mass of any nuclide shown. It follows that energy will be released by any fusion process in which other light nuclei react and give ^{4}He as the product. The last column gives the energy, in terajoules per kilogram, which would be released if one could in practice achieve the transmutation of each nuclide into ^{4}He.

Some feasible fusion processes are shown in Table 9. ^{4}He is, indeed, the main product in most of the cases, and it is worth noting that for this reason the word 'fusion' is often a misnomer. For example, the reaction

$$H + {}^7Li \rightarrow 2 \cdot {}^4He$$

is more like the fission of lithium than fusion; nevertheless it is conventional to speak of fusion where any of these light elements are concerned. Table 9 includes the energy output (in MeV, see 'Units') from each reaction, except in the case of one reaction which is initiated by a neutron and will be discussed later below.

Table 9 *Some fusion reactions*

Reaction					Energy output (MeV)
D	+	D	→	T	+ H	4.0
D	+	D	→	^{3}He	+ n	3.2
D	+	T	→	^{4}He	+ n	17.6
D	+	^{3}He	→	^{4}He	+ H	18.3
n	+	^{6}Li	→	^{4}He	+ T	(tritium 'breeding')
H	+	^{6}Li	→	^{4}He	+ ^{3}He	4.0
D	+	^{6}Li	→	2.^{4}He		22.4
D	+	^{6}Li	→	^{7}Li	+ H	5.0
^{3}He	+	^{6}Li	→	2.^{4}He	+ H	16.9
H	+	^{7}Li	→	2.^{4}He		17.5
H	+	^{11}B	→	3.^{4}He		8.7

The first two reactions in Table 9, the DD reactions, have the advantage that the deuterium used can be got in inexhaustible supply from seawater. Unfortunately, DD fusion is technically very difficult to achieve, requiring an ignition temperature in the hundreds of millions of degrees Celsius. By far the most promising reaction is the DT process (third in the list) which can be ignited at about 40 million degrees. This is still an enormous temperature, of course, and the main aim of fusion power research is to sustain such a temperature together with adequate pressure and density for a time sufficient for DT fusion to take place on a useful scale. Assuming that DT fusion is achieved, the supply of the tritium may become a problem. Tritium does not occur in nature, as it decays with a 12-year half-life: one way of manufacturing it is by bombarding lithium (in particular, ^{6}Li) with neutrons. This tritium 'breeding' could in principle be achieved by neutrons from a fission reactor by the neutrons which are a by-product of DT fusion itself.

The dependence on lithium as a source of tritium may, conceivably, be a constraint on the exploitation of fusion power. It is more likely, though, that more sophisticated fusion fuels like ^{11}B will come into use before then, or perhaps that a fusion energy system based only on deuterium will have been devised. See also **fusion reactors, fuel pellets, muon catalysed fusion, inertial confinement, impact fusion, binding energy, nuclear fuel cycles.**

fusion reactors   Devices which have been proposed and one day may be built to exploit nuclear fusion energy in a controlled way. Since they require enormous temperatures for the reacting plasma, the main design difficulty is in the containment of the plasma, and different approaches to this problem have led to two main classes of fusion reactor concept. One, termed 'magnetic confinement', is based on the use of a shaped magnetic field to confine the hot plasma within a vessel which is usually toroidal, or doughnut-shaped. The other is 'inertial confinement', which is not really confinement at all but rather the reckoning that a small quantity of fusible matter, heated and compressed very rapidly, might stay together for long enough to provide a useful energy yield before blowing itself apart.

Magnetic confinement technology is now advancing rapidly, and a number of experimental devices have been or are being built. A working reactor in the future may have many of the features illustrated in Figure 20. The reactor body is torus-shaped, with a reacting plasma of deuterium and tritium in a central cavity free of air. The neutrons given off by the fusion reactions can be absorbed in a lithium 'blanket' in which tritium will be produced. That is surrounded

65

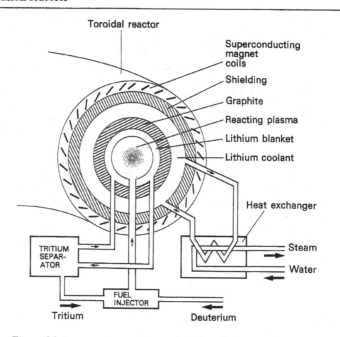

Figure 20 A magnetic confinement nuclear fusion reactor.

by a layer of graphite which acts as a neutron shield, and that in turn is surrounded by a lithium coolant layer connected to an external steam circuit for the generation of electricity. Outside the coolant layer there is shielding against radiation and heat, and then come the magnet coils whose field actually controls the motion of the plasma in the centre. The magnets would be super-conducting so as to give a powerful field without taking up too much electrical power: consequently, cryogenic technology is involved.

Figure 21 shows the principles of an inertial confinement fusion reactor in which **fuel pellets** are heated and compressed by a battery of laser or heavy-ion beams. The necessary high temperature is achieved because of the high power of the beams and the small size of the pellets, which are released in quick succession and would have to be guided into the path of the beams by an active control system (not illustrated). As in the case of the previous figure, the reactor vessel is cooled by a flow of lithium which raises steam through a heat exchanger.

There are a host of other, less well developed, concepts associated

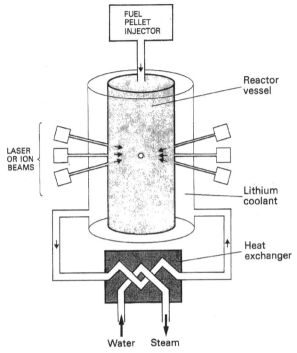

Figure 21 An intertial confinement nuclear fusion reactor.

with nuclear fusion power, such as **impact fusion** and **muon catalysed fusion**. See also **nuclear fuel cycles**.

gallium arsenide   A semiconducting material which is an alternative to silicon for the manufacture of photovoltaic solar cells. Gallium arsenide (GaAs) cells can support higher voltages, but at lower current, than silicon; higher efficiencies may be attainable with GaAs, but at present silicon appears more promising because of its relative cheapness. See also **photovoltaic cells**.

gamma-radiation The form of **electromagnetic radiation** which can be given off by a nucleus after a radioactive decay or nuclear reaction. Gamma-rays have extremely short wavelengths, of the order of nuclear sizes, and so they are of high energy per quantum. Gamma-rays are sufficiently penetrating to be biologically hazardous and to degrade the structure of many materials after prolonged exposure.

gas Colloquially, 'gas' may be an abbreviation of 'gasoline' or may refer to gas piped as a domestic fuel (mostly **methane**). In addition there are many other gases used as fuels for special purposes, e.g. acetylene, hydrogen and propane.

gas centrifuge A system for the enrichment of uranium. Uranium hexafluoride gas (UF_6) is spun in a centrifuge fast enough for the heavier isotope of uranium to be partially separated from the lighter isotope. The degree of separation is tiny, but by passing samples of UF_6 through a cascade of centrifuges it is possible to build up a quantity of uranium highly enriched in the valuable light isotope.

gas-cooled fast breeder reactor (GCFR).

gas turbine A type of engine frequently used for small-scale electricity generation or for propulsion, and usually powered by a liquid fuel. See also **turbine**.

gaseous diffusion A system for uranium enrichment which, like the gas centrifuge, acts on uranium in the form of the gas UF_6, i.e. uranium hexafluoride. The UF_6 will diffuse through a porous material, but the rate of diffusion for molecules with a lighter ^{235}U atom is greater than for ^{235}U, because at a fixed temperature the lighter molecules will be moving more quickly. The difference in diffusion rates is very small, but by letting samples of the gas diffuse repeatedly in several stages effective enrichment can be achieved.

gasification The manufacture of a gaseous fuel, which may be largely composed of hydrogen, carbon monoxide and methane, from coal. It may be done simply because gas is more convenient to handle than coal, or because gas can be used directly in a gas turbine (see for example **fluidised bed combustion**). Another type of idea is to gasify unmined coal *in situ* as a way of exploiting otherwise unrecoverable deposits of coal.

gasohol A mixture of ordinary automobile fuel, i.e. gasoline, with 10 per cent or thereabouts of alcohol. The alcohol is usually biologically-derived ethanol, and so gasohol can be regarded as a way of conserving oil by using a form of solar energy. See also **biological energy**.

gasoline The common term in the USA for ordinary automobile fuel, mostly hydrocarbons with between 5 and 10 carbon atoms to each molecule. Its calorific value is about 47 MJ/kg.

GCFR Gas-cooled fast breeder reactor. See **nuclear reactors**.

generator A machine for converting rotary motion into electric power, in an inverse fashion to an electric motor. The generator works on the principle that a current will be induced in a conducting wire which moves across a magnetic field. The attainable energy efficiency is very high, and so generators figure in various schemes for energy storage, of which the flywheel is one example.

geothermal energy The energy manifest in the natural upflowing heat of the earth.

It is now understood that geothermal energy has its source in the decay heat of certain radioactive isotopes in the crust of the earth, isotopes having half-lives comparable to the age of the earth. The isotopes responsible are for the most part of thorium (^{232}Th) and uranium (^{238}U and to some extent ^{235}U). See figures 22 and 23. Of the earth's total mass of 6×10^{24} kg, something like one part in ten million is of thorium, which produces decay heat at a rate of about 30 μW/kg. Uranium is equally important: there is less of it than thorium, but in compensation it gives more decay heat (100 μW/kg). Together, these two metals are constantly generating in the region of 30 terawatts of power. One or two other processes may also be contributing to geothermal energy, such as tidal friction within the earth itself or a gravitational contraction of the earth, but their role is uncertain and controversial.

The 30 terawatts are sufficient to maintain the high temperature of the earth's interior, and hence continuing geological activity (in contrast to some other planets in the solar system). The power flows up to the surface, there amounting to an average of around 60 milliwatts per square metre, but with wide variations according to local geological conditions. This means that under a large house there may be as much energy flowing up as would light an electric bulb continuously. This is several thousand times less than the radiant energy flow down from the sun.

However, there are two types of circumstance in which geothermal energy can be tapped abundantly and profitably. First, one can go to those parts of the world (Iceland is a well-known example)

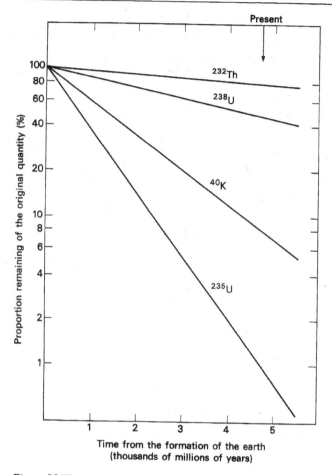

Figure 22 The decay of radioactive isotopes in the earth.

where special conditions lead to a heat flow many times greater than the average. In especially favoured spots hot springs supply a constant source of energy more than adequate for local needs. Unfortunately, such areas are very unusual and it is not conceivable that they could ever be used to supply a significant proportion of total world energy demand.

The second approach is the drilling of very deep boreholes. Almost everywhere, geothermal heat leads to a temperature rising with

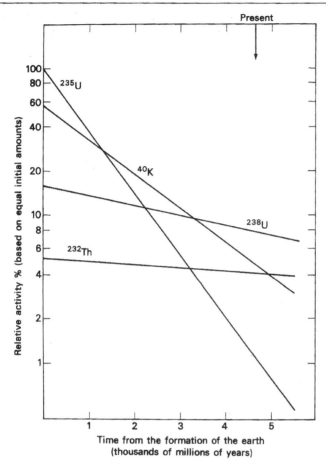

Figure 23 The activities of radioisotopes in the earth since its formation.

depth at a rate of the order of 25 C per kilometre. Thus, there will often be rocks at above 100 C four kilometres or so down. There are various techniques by which flows of water can be used to bring that heat to the surface; the cost of doing so will depend on the depth chosen, the porosity and strength of the rock, and whether or not there is a pre-existing deposit of water at that depth, as well as other factors. It is important to realise that geothermal energy of this kind is not really a 'renewable' resource, since the slow rate of conduction

71

up from further below will not nearly match the artificial extraction of heat from a borehole. Any particular borehole will only be good for a certain limited amount of energy, and once it begins to run cool it may take years or decades lying fallow for the original high temperature to re-establish itself. Nevertheless, rapid technological progress with deep-boring and rock-fracturing methods give good reason for hope that geothermal energy will have a significant long-term future in the extraction of deep-lying heat at points all over the world.

geovoltaic energy   Electrical power extracted directly from the earth, exploiting the fact that substantial voltage gradients may occur because of variations in chemical composition and, more importantly, temperature gradients within the earth. Geovoltaic energy is best thought of as a natural **Seebeck effect.**

Gibbs free energy   Sometimes called the 'free enthalpy', this is a thermodynamic potential function given by

$$G = U + p \cdot V - T \cdot S$$

where U is the internal energy of the substance concerned (usually a gas); and p, V, T, and S are its pressure, volume, temperature and entropy.

gigawatt (GW)   A rate of energy production (or consumption) equal to 1,000 megawatts; see 'Units'. The capacity of a large central electricity generating plant might typically be around 1 gigawatt.

gobar gas   A name used, especially in India, for the gas produced by small biodigesters fed by agricultural refuse. Gobar gas is predominantly methane.

graphite   A form of carbon, graphite is used as a moderator in certain types of nuclear fission reactor.

gravitation   The universal force by which all matter is mutually attracted. It is responsible for the gross, large-scale features of the universe. Although the dominant force for large aggregations of matter, gravitation on the small scale is much weaker and only in a few special cases can it be used as a source of energy. One case is **tidal energy,** and another is **hydroelectricity,** and in both these instances gravitational energy is converted into electricity by letting water fall under gravity through turbines. Water falling through, say, 10 metres will yield less than 100 joules per kilogram.

Gravitation is, of course, the main constraint on transport between the earth's surface and space; about 60 MJ/kg are needed to overcome it.

gray (Gy) The standard unit by which doses of **radiation** are measured. The gray corresponds to an energy deposition of 1 J/kg and so is 100 times larger than the older, more familiar, unit the **rad**.

greenhouse effect The phenomenon whereby the atmosphere lets solar energy, which is mainly in the form of visible light, pass through it to the surface, while the heat thereby produced at ground level is 'trapped' because it is radiated at infra-red wavelengths to which the atmosphere is almost opaque. The atmosphere's opacity to infra-red radiation is due in large measure to its carbon dioxide content. It can therefore be said, although it is an oversimplification, that carbon dioxide traps the heat from the sun and leads to a high surface temperature on the earth.

half-life Any radioactive substance decays away in such a fashion that equal time intervals reduce it by equal proportions. The time interval which reduces the quantity by half is the 'half-life' and is a characteristic of the particular substance.

In symbols,

$$N_B/N_A = 2^{(t_A - t_B)/t_{1/2}}$$

where N_A and N_B are the numbers of nuclei of a substance present in a sample at times t_A and t_B respectively, and $t_{1/2}$ is the substance's half-life. From this formula one can see that when the time interval $t_B - t_A$ is equal to the half-life $t_{1/2}$ then the ratio N_B/N_A is equal to ½. When the interval is twice the half-life, the ratio is a quarter; when the interval is three half-lives, the ratio is an eighth; when the interval is four half-lives, the ratio is a sixteenth; and so on. See Figures 22 and 23 under **geothermal energy**.

Instead of the half-life, one sometimes uses the 'mean life' or average life: denoting it by t_M we have

$$N_B/N_A = \exp(-(t_B - t_A)/t_M)$$

and

73

$$t_{\frac{1}{2}} = t_M \cdot \ln 2 \qquad (\ln 2 = 0.693)$$

For example, the half-life of the neutron is 11 minutes, and so the average lifetime of a neutron is about 15 minutes: of any sample of neutrons, 99.9 will have decayed after an interval of ten half-lives, i.e. 2 hours. See also **exponential**.

Hanford   Site in Washington State, USA, where the first plutonium-producing nuclear reactor was built during the Second World War. Hanford is an extensive nuclear-industrial complex which now includes storage for a very large volume of radioactive waste.

haybox   The 'haybox' principle is the use of heavy insulation to enable an oven to operate at high temperature over a long time with only a small input of power.

halocarbon   An organic compound which consists mostly of carbon and halogen atoms; the halogen elements are fluorine, chlorine, bromine and iodine. Compounds of fluorine and chlorine with carbon are important as **refrigerants**.

hard coal   Any of the higher grades of coal containing, say, more than 60 per cent carbon by weight.

heat   Energy which is in the form of the random motion of individual atoms or molecules. Heat, in other words, is microscopic kinetic energy.

heat capacity   Otherwise known as 'specific heat', this is the amount of heat energy needed to raise the temperature of one kilogram of a substance by one degree. The heat capacity of anything will vary somewhat with temperature, and the figures tabulated correspond to normal room temperature except in the cases of ice (0 C) and steam (100 C).

For heavy elements, the heat capacity tends to fall in inverse proportion to the atomic weight or atomic mass number (A) of the element. This gives a useful rule for calculating the heat capacities of many materials, i.e.:

heat capacity $\times$ atomic mass number $= 25$ kJ/kg/K

See also **heat storage**.

heat exchanger   Any device which enables heat to flow from one medium into another, cooler, medium. This is achieved by bringing the two close together, separated only by a thin partition with a

Table 10 *Heat capacities*

Substance	Heat capacity (kJ/kg/K)
Air	1.01
Aluminium	0.90
Copper	0.38
Ice	2.10
Iron	0.45
Lead	0.13
Nitrogen	1.04
Silicon	0.71
Steam	1.95
Water	4.20

large surface area and good conduction properties.

For example, at the back of most refrigerators is a heat exchanger by which the refrigerant fluid sheds heat through metal piping to the surrounding air.

heat pipe A kind of pipe which can be used to transfer heat from one place to another; to be exact, it is **latent heat** that is transferred, a liquid moving one way along the pipe and its vapour moving the other way. A heat pipe will consist of a hollow centre along which the vapour is led, surrounded by a fibrous layer to conduct the liquid by capillary action, and outside that a covering of insulating material. An important design consideration is the selection of a suitable fluid given the temperature at which the heat pipe is to be used.

heat pump A device which extracts heat from a body at one temperature and transfers it to another at a higher temperature. A heat pump therefore goes against the 'natural' tendency for heat to flow from warm bodies to cool ones.

A heat pump can operate only because it uses energy (often in the form of electricity) supplied in addition to the heat it pumps. If the energy supplied is E, then

$$Q_1 + E = Q_2$$

where Q_1 is the heat absorbed at the lower temperature T_1, and Q_2 is that given out at the higher temperature T_2. The ratio of heat out to energy supplied is known as the 'coefficient of performance', or COP:

$$COP = Q_2/E$$

and for a heat pump based on a thermodynamical cycle there is a fundamental limitation given by

$$COP < T_1 / (T_2 - T_1)$$

In practice, heat pumps operate at well below this theoretically attainable COP, with values around 2 or 3 being usual.

The most familiar heat pumps are those used in domestic refrigerators, using the **vapour compression cycle**. This same device is also the basis of many heat pumps used in heating and air conditioning. Other kinds of heat pump are the **absorption cycle** heat pump, the **chemical heat pump**, and others based on **thermoelectricity**.

For many reasons one can expect a rapid increase in heat-pump use in the future. The pressure towards energy conservation is making heat pumps viable economically in circumstances where they were previously not worth while; improvements in electric motor technology are making the theoretical maximum COP less unattainable; and heat pumps run by solar heat or by combustion engines can avoid the inherent inefficiency of using centrally-generated electricity.

heat recovery   Any of a wide range of techniques used to conserve energy by usefully using heat which would otherwise be rejected and lost. As just one example, Figure 24 shows how a refrigeration system can be linked with a water-heating system so as to reduce the energy which will be consumed by the latter. There are now many arrangements of this kind which are well worth implementing on the industrial, if not domestic, scale.

heat storage   In many circumstances, including some **domestic energy** systems, it is useful to store heat in material chosen for its high thermal or latent heat capacity. For example, water in a well-insulated tank can be used to store heat for long periods, and it is feasible with thick insulation and a large basement tank to retain heat from the summer right through into the winter.

It is important to distinguish between 'sensible' heat, i.e. which makes the storage medium get hotter and hotter, and latent heat which goes into melting the medium without changing its temperature. Table 11 shows heat capacities of both kinds.

heat wheel   A device used in industrial heat recovery which transfers heat from one stream of gas to another. Hot gas from, say, a combustion engine exhaust is passed through one side of a metal mesh wheel; the air-stream to be heated passes through the other side. Rotation of the wheel then transfers a valuable amount of heat.

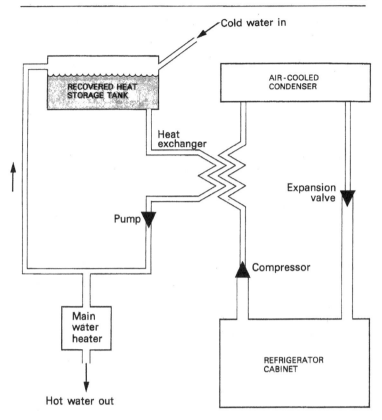

Figure 24 A heat recovery system. Heat given off by a refrigerator, instead of being lost, is used to preheat water.

Table 11 *Heat storage capacities*

Material	Latent heat (MJ/kg)	Sensible heat (kJ/kg/K)
Potassium fluoride solution (melts 18 C)	0.23	
Calcium chloride solution (melts 29 C)	0.17	
Water (melts 0 C)	0.33	4.2
Wet soil		3
Dry soil		1
Concrete, bricks, etc.		1

77

heavy water (D_2O)   Water in which the hydrogen atoms are of the heavy isotope, deuterium. Because deuterium does not absorb neutrons as readily as ordinary hydrogen, heavy water is an effective moderator in nuclear fission reactors. It is used, for example, in the **CANDU** design.

heliohydroelectricity   A form of hydroelectricity in which the head of water is maintained not by rain or river water into an upper reservoir but by solar evaporation from a lower reservoir. It has been proposed, for example, that desert depressions below sea level in North Africa could be linked by pipeline to the Mediterranean: power could be generated by the seawater flowing down, while solar heat would prevent the depression from ever filling up.

heliostat   A mechanism for keeping a directional solar energy collector pointed in the right direction as the sun moves across the sky.

helium   The element (symbol He) with atomic number $Z = 2$. Natural helium (which is found as a small proportion in natural gas) consists almost entirely of the isotope ^4He. The ^4He nucleus contains two protons and two neutrons in an extremely stable configuration and is the same thing as an alpha-particle.

   Being a light, non-reactive gas, not prone to absorbing neutrons, helium is useful as a coolant in certain types of nuclear fission reactor.

   A lighter isotope of helium, ^3He, which is stable but occurs hardly at all in nature, could be useful as a secondary nuclear fusion fuel in the distant future.

Helmholtz free energy (or just 'free energy')   A thermodynamic potential function given by

$$F = U - T \cdot S$$

where U is the energy of a system as normally defined, T is its temperature and S its entropy.

hex   Short for uranium hexafluoride (UF_6), a gaseous compound which is especially convenient in the separation of the two isotopes of natural uranium. See **gaseous diffusion**, **gas centrifuge**.

high-grade heat   Heat at high temperature. A given amount of energy may appear either as a large mass at low temperature or as a small mass at a higher temperature; although the amounts of energy may be the same the latter is generally more useful and is so regarded as a higher 'grade' of heat.

high-temperature gas-cooled reactor   See HTGR.

horsepower (hp)   A unit traditionally used to measure the rate of working of an engine of any kind, i.e. to measure power. One horsepower is equal to 746 watts. See 'Units'.

HP   See horsepower.

HTGR   High-temperature gas-cooled reactor. A type of **nuclear reactor** cooled by a gas such as helium and able to achieve a temperature well above that of a water-cooled reactor.

HTR   High-temperature reactor. See **nuclear reactors**.

hydraulic fracturing   A method of fracturing rocks deep underground so as to make them more porous. The procedure permits more efficient extraction of oil, gas or hot water from underground reservoirs. Hydraulic fracturing is carried out by pumping a fluid down a borehole under very high pressure.

hydrocarbon   Any compound of hydrogen and carbon. Crude oil, natural gas and their derivatives are almost pure hydrocarbons, as are hydrogen and carbon themselves. The hydrocarbons number thousands of different compounds, many of which are constituents of widely-used fuels. See also **fuel**.

hydroelectricity   Electric power generated from a flow of water. Hydroelectric systems vary over a wide range in scale, from those based on turbines in small rivers up to those driven from massive artificial lakes. Hydroelectricity represents a method of electricity production which is clean and free of waste heat production, and it is a renewable energy source replenished by the natural hydrological cycle. Moreover, hydroelectricity can meet a fluctuating demand. On the debit side, hydroelectric schemes may demand enormous capital investment and their environmental impact can be heavy.

   Hydroelectricity accounts for about 20 EJ of energy annually, i.e. some 6 per cent of the world's energy consumption.

hydrofracturing   See hydraulic fracturing.

hydrogen   The simplest of the elements, having atomic number $Z = 1$ (symbol H). Hydrogen comes in three different isotopes, of which the most common by far is ^{1}H, with a nucleus consisting of a proton alone. The second isotope (^{2}H or D) is deuterium, a stable nuclide that may be valuable as a nuclear fusion fuel; and the third isotope is tritium (^{3}H, or T), which is a radioactive nuclide with a half-life of 12.3 years. Like deuterium, tritium may have a role to play as a nuclear fusion fuel.

Hydrogen is a combustible gas which may be used as a fuel, having a calorific value of 121 MJ/kg. It has been proposed as a secondary fuel on which a whole economy might be based, with hydrogen being used as a universal fuel and produced (e.g. electrolytically from water) on a very large scale.

As an alternative to storing hydrogen as a gas or as a pressurised liquid, it is possible to combine it with certain metals in solid form. These 'hydrides' are promising as a fuel-storage system for vehicles in the future.

hydrological cycle   The natural cycle by which water is evaporated from the surface of the oceans, transported in the atmosphere, is precipitated, and flows down rivers to the seas. The hydrological cycle is driven by the energy of the sun, and can itself be tapped for power as in the case of hydroelectricity.

hygas   A process for the gasification of coal which involves applying a hot stream of hydrogen-rich gas to the crushed coal. Finally a methane-rich fuel gas is produced.

IAEA   The International Atomic Energy Agency, formed in 1957 under the auspices of the United Nations and charged with the promotion of nuclear energy for peaceful purposes. The IAEA acts as an information centre, it sponsors research, and it has responsibilities in the implementation of the nuclear Non-Proliferation Treaty. The IAEA has about 110 member nations, and an annual budget which in 1976 was close to US$ 35m.

ICRP   The International Commission on Radiological Protection, a group of scientists first founded in 1928 which has published information and recommendations concerning the effects of radiation and the dosages which might be tolerable.

impact fusion   A proposed method of achieving controlled nuclear fusion by magnetically accelerating tiny metallic pellets to very high speeds (of the order of 100 km/s) and letting them strike a solid wall whose surface contains a suitable mixture of fusion fuels. The temperature and pressure created by the impact may bring about fusion briefly, leading to an overall energy gain.

induction heating   A method of indirect electric heating, whereby an arrangement of current-carrying coils induces an oscillating magnetic field in the interior of whatever is to be heated. The field in turn drives 'eddy currents' which are dissipated into the required heat. Induction heating is widely used for melting metal.

inertial confinement   When a nuclear fusion fuel is used it has to be confined at high temperature and pressure for a certain length of time. Inertial confinement systems achieve this by using high-energy beams to heat a small sample of fuel which then undergoes fusion before it has time to blow apart. See also **fusion reactors.**

infra-red   Electromagnetic radiation with frequency lying below that of the red end of the visible light spectrum. The infra-red wavelength range is taken to be 0.75 to 1,000 microns. Any hot object will radiate energy over a wavelength range peaking at approximately

  wavelength peak $= 2900/T$ microns,

where T is its temperature in degrees Kelvin. For everyday temperatures (say, $T = 300$ K), the wavelength peak is in the infra-red.

insolation   The radiation received on the earth's surface from the sun. See also **solar energy**.

Institute for Energy Analysis   Centre at **Oak Ridge**, Tennessee, USA, for energy research.

insulation   The containment of heat energy by materials chosen for their low heat conductivity. See also **U-value.**

internal combustion engine (ICE)   Any kind of engine in which a fuel burns in a combustion chamber producing a hot gas which is directly used to drive a mechanism. The ICE is to be distinguished from external combustion engines such as the Stirling engine or the old-fashioned steam engine.

International Atomic Energy Agency   See **IAEA.**

International Commission on Radiological Protection　See **ICRP**.

iodine　An element formed at a fission product in nuclear reactors. There are several beta-active isotopes, of which one, ^{131}I, has a half-life of 8 days and can constitute a health hazard. Iodine can be taken up into the natural food chain and in humans will be concentrated into the thyroid gland.

ion　An atom or molecule which is not electrically neutral, i.e. in which the positive charge of the nucleus or nuclei is not exactly balanced by the number of electrons. Matter in bulk is always electrically neutral (otherwise enormous electric forces would build up) and so positive ions are usually to be found in close association with negative ions or free electrons.

ion-beam fusion　Ionised atoms, being charged, can be accelerated to very high energies by electromagnetic fields. Beams of accelerated ions can be used to focus intense energy onto a small object in a very short time, and this has been proposed as a way of igniting fusion in nuclear fusion fuel pellets.

ionising radiation　Radiation of any kind which is sufficiently energetic to strip electrons from their atomic orbits, forming ions.

isentropic　In thermodynamics, an isentropic process is one which takes place without change in **entropy**, i.e. a process which is reversible and **adiabatic**.

isomer　(1) A pair of chemical compounds are isomeric if they have the same atoms in their molecules but arranged in a different way. For example, butane (C_4H_{10}) is a hydrocarbon with its four carbon atoms in a chain, and it has the isomer isobutane in which they make up a branched chain.

(2) In nuclear physics, it is possible for two kinds of nuclei to have the same composition in terms of proton and neutron numbers but to have slightly different energies and to decay in different ways. They are then called 'isomers'. The lead isotope ^{207}Pb is stable and abundant, but it has an isomer (also denoted ^{207}Pb) decaying by gamma-ray emission with a half-life of just under a second.

isothermal　At constant temperature. The term is most often used to describe stages in heat engine cycles during which the working fluid is neither heated nor cooled. An example is the evaporation stage in a refrigerator, during which the fluid absorbs energy and vaporises without temperature change.

isotope   All chemical elements may occur in different nuclear forms, the nucleus containing different numbers of neutrons. These forms are the isotopes of the element. For example, the element carbon has a nucleus with six protons and either four, five, six, seven, eight or nine neutrons, so that there are isotopes ^{10}C, ^{11}C, ^{12}C, ^{13}C, ^{14}C and ^{15}C. Of these, only two (^{12}C and ^{13}C) are stable, the others decaying radioactively.

isotopic power generator   A device to generate electrical power from the decay heat of a sample of a radioactive isotope. Since the isotope may be long-lived, such generators may be designed to give power without refuelling over a long period of time, and have been used to power spacecraft communications, navigational buoys, etc.

Examples of isotopic power generator fuels are cobalt (^{60}Co, yielding 5.3 kW kg^{-1} over a half-life of 5.3 years) and plutonium (^{238}Pu, yielding 0.4 kW kg^{-1} over a half-life of 86 years).

JET   The Joint European Torus, a machine being built near Culham, for research on nuclear fusion through the magnetic confinement of hot plasma.

jet engine   A propulsion system in which a vehicle is pushed forward by the reaction against a stream of gas ejected at very high pressure from behind the vehicle. A special type of jet engine is the rocket, in which the gas is the residue of combustion of a fuel which burns without any external oxygen supply. Jet engines used in aircraft are of many different types (ramjet, turbojet, etc.), but work to the same principle: air drawn in at the front is used to burn fuel, producing a hot, high-pressure exhaust which provides thrust for the vehicle.

joule (J)   The unit of energy in the conventional SI (metre-kilogram-second) system; see 'Units'. A joule is equal to the energy dissipated by an electrical current of 1 ampere driven by 1 volt for 1 second; it is also equal to twice the energy of motion in a mass of 1 kilogram moving at 1 metre per second.

K-capture   A form of radioactive decay whereby an atomic nucleus first absorbs an electron from among the atom's orbiting electrons and subsequently radiates a neutrino. It is akin to **beta-decay**. One example is the decay of an isotope of beryllium, ^{7}Be, into one of lithium. Another example is provided by the actinide metal mendelevium, all of whose isotopes may decay in this way into isotopes of fermium.

Kelvin   The scale of **temperature**, also known as the 'absolute' scale, whose zero point is at **absolute zero** and whose degrees are of the same magnitude as those of the **Celsius** scale. A temperature in degrees Kelvin (K) can be converted to degrees Celsius by subtracting 273. It should be remembered that most fundamental physical formulae involving temperature (such as the Stefan–Boltzmann law) require the use of Kelvin temperatures.

kerosine   A fuel derived from petroleum and used mainly for jet propulsion or for small heaters. Its calorific value is about 48 MJ/kg. In Britain it is usually known as paraffin.

kilowatt (kW)   The unit of power equal to 1,000 watts, i.e. to 1 kilojoule per second; see 'Units'. Typically, an electric fire might use energy at a rate of 1 kilowatt.

kilowatt-hour (kWh)   This is the quantity of energy passing each hour through a device with a power of 1 kilowatt. A kilowatt-hour is equal to 3.6 MJ, because by definition a watt-second is a joule.

kinetic energy   The energy which any moving object can be said to possess by virtue of its motion. If the object has a mass m (in kilograms) and velocity v (in metres per second) then its kinetic energy in joules is given by

$$KE = \tfrac{1}{2} mv^2$$

except when v is comparable with the speed of light c, when a more exact formula is

$$KE = 2mc^2 \cdot \sinh^2 (\tfrac{1}{2}y).$$

Here y is a new variable called the 'rapidity', such that

$$v = c \cdot \tanh (y).$$

Kirchoff's law   The rate at which a body gives off radiant energy is proportional to the absorptivity of its surface. It must be remembered, however, that both the radiation and absorption may vary somewhat with wavelength and temperature. A consequence of the law is that the **absorptivity** of a surface is equal to its **emissivity**.

krypton   A gas having low thermal conductivity which is inserted instead of air between panes of glass in some multiple glazing systems. It is a rare gas, occurring in the atmosphere at the level of just over one part per million by volume.

laser   A device, energy-efficient but sophisticated, which can produce electromagnetic radiation at optical wavelengths in an intense, monochromatic, coherent beam. Such beams, carrying large amounts of energy to a small area in an extremely short time, can give rise to very high temperatures momentarily. In this way lasers can be used to trigger nuclear fusion by a system which is of promise as an energy generation system for the long-term future.

   Another application of lasers is known as 'laser enrichment', and is concerned with the separation of the light isotope of uranium (^{235}U) from natural uranium (preponderantly ^{238}U). Although chemical methods are normally inadequate for this separation, lasers can be tuned in wavelength with sufficient precision that laser-stimulated chemical processes may be used to enrich uranium in spite of the close similarity between the chemistries of ^{235}U and ^{238}U.

latent heat   When a substance melts, boils, sublimes, condenses, freezes or vaporises there is a flow of heat involved. This is known as 'latent' heat since the change of state does not in itself involve a change in temperature, and the heat may seem to be 'hidden'.

   For example, at body temperature water has a latent heat of vaporisation equal to 2.4 MJ/kg, and since an average person might

85

sweat about 30 g of water per hour this amounts to a shedding of energy at a rate of about 20 watts, although there will be no change in temperature. See also **heat storage**.

lawrencium (symbol Lr)   The heaviest of the actinide metals and the element of atomic number $Z = 103$.

lead (symbol Pb)   The element of atomic number $Z = 82$, a soft but heavy metal important because of its widespread use in the electrodes of lead-acid storage cells such as those used in automobiles. It has been pointed out that lead supplies would be a limiting factor in any widespread replacement of the internal combustion engine by electric motors powered by lead-acid storage cells, and for this and other reasons there is intensive research under way to develop cells based on substances other than lead.

Leclanché cell   A kind of electric **storage cell** providing electric power through the action of an ammonium chloride electrolyte on electrodes of zinc and manganese dioxide.

lepton   A member of the family of fundamental particles which includes electrons and neutrinos. Leptons are not influenced by the ordinary nuclear forces but are produced in radioactive beta-decay.

light   Visible light consists of electromagnetic radiation with wavelength in a certain range of the spectrum, i.e. between 0.4 and 0.7 microns. This corresponds to energies between 0.3 and 0.5 aJ per quantum.

light-water reactor   See **LWR**.

lignite   Otherwise called 'brown coal', a fossil fuel of comparatively low calorific value (about 14 MJ/kg). See also **fossil fuels**.

liquefied natural gas (LNG)   Natural gas, i.e. mostly methane (CH_4), kept as a liquid under pressure for bulk transportation or storage. The convenience of liquefied natural gas is partly offset by the energy required to liquefy it and by the danger inherent in handling a highly flammable fuel under pressure.

liquid-metal-cooled fast breeder reactor   See **LMFBR**

liquified petroleum gas (LPG)   (Note that the 'i' in 'liquified' is conventional in this phrase.) LPG is gas derived from oil, usually propane or butane, under pressure so that it is in liquid form. Canisters of LPG are often used to power portable cooking-stoves or heaters.

lithium   The third element in the periodic table, with atomic number $Z = 3$ and symbol Li. Lithium is a light metal and is fairly common, occurring with isotopes ^{6}Li (7.4%) and ^{7}Li (92.6%). It may be of value in the future for **fusion** energy, and the lighter isotope in particular is useful because of the reaction

$$n + {}^6Li \rightarrow {}^3H + {}^4He$$

by which it can absorb neutrons to give the fusion fuel tritium with helium as a by-product.

lithium anode cell   An electrical **storage cell** of which one electrode is made of the metal lithium. The other electrode, the cathode, is a mixture of iodine and poly-2-vinylpyridine (P2VP), and the electrolyte is solid lithium iodide. Such batteries are used in heart pacemakers.

lithium deuteride   A compound of lithium (to be precise, the lighter isotope ^{6}Li) with heavy hydrogen (i.e. deuterium), which acts as a potent fusion fuel in nuclear weapons. Under irradiation by neutrons the lithium gives rise to tritium by the process mentioned under **lithium**, while the deuterium (^{2}H) fuses with the tritium with a heavy release of energy. Fusion weapons proliferation has been considered as a danger which might arise from the widespread use of fusion for energy production in the future.

LMFBR   Liquid-metal-cooled fast breeder reactor, a kind of **nuclear reactor** that uses cycles of the liquid metal sodium as coolant. An example is the French Phénix reactor.

LNG   See **liquefied natural gas**.

LOCA   Loss-of-coolant accident, one of the main operational risks of nuclear fission reactors, whereby excessive heating of the reactor core might occur if the coolant (usually circulating steam or pressurised water) were accidentally cut off. Reactors are generally designed with elaborate precautions against LOCAs.

LPG   See **liquefied petroleum gas**.

Lurgi process   The original process by which coal, treated with steam and oxygen under pressure, can give rise to a gaseous fuel composed for the most part of methane. The fuel is today often referred to as **synthetic natural gas.**

LWBR   Light-water breeder reactor. See **nuclear reactors.**

LWR   Light-water reactor. A **nuclear reactor** using ordinary water (H_2O) as the primary core coolant.

magnetic confinement   In nuclear fusion, this is the use of magnetic fields to contain and insulate a hot reacting plasma whose temperature may be of the order of tens of millions of degrees. See also **fusion reactors.**

magnetism   Closely related to electric forces; see **electromagnetism.** A magnetic field will impose a force on an electric current, this being the principle of the electric motor. Plasmas (i.e. gases heated to the point of dissociating electrically and becoming conducting) can be manipulated magnetically; this has led to the technology of magnetohydrodynamics. The earth itself has a magnetic field amounting to an energy density of between 0.25 (equator) and 1.7 (poles) mJ m^{-3} just above the earth's surface.

magnetohydrodynamics (MHD)   The technology by which magnetic fields may be used to control the flow of an ionised fluid, especially gas at very high temperature. MHD has two main applications to energy conversion. One of its uses is to confine plasma in some proposed types of nuclear **fusion reactor,** and the other is to obtain some electric power directly from the hot gas produced by fossil fuel combustion.

Both these applications are still largely experimental, but in the latter case demonstration plant have produced power. The principle is fairly straightforward; combustion produces a jet of gas at sufficiently high temperature to be ionised, and it passes across a magnetic field which deflects positive ions one way and negative ions the other. This separation of charge gives a voltage from which electrical power can be got, while the gas continues at slightly reduced speed to raise steam for a conventional turbine.

MAGNOX   A kind of gas-cooled nuclear fission reactor developed in the UK, so called because of the magnesium alloy used to clad the uranium fuel. See **nuclear reactors.**

manioc   A crop common in Brazil which can be used to produce alcohol as a fuel by fermentation. See **biological energy.**

maser   A device to produce microwave radiation by the same principle as the laser. The name is an acronym for Microwave Amplification by Stimulated Emission of Radiation.

mass   A property which, in the context of relativity theory, is known to be interchangeable with energy at the rate of 90 PJ kg^{-1}. However, no practicable method exists for turning more than a tiny fraction of a fuel's mass into radiant energy, because of the conservation of baryons.

mass number   The total number of nucleons, i.e. protons and neutrons together, in an atomic nucleus. The mass number (symbol A) ranges from 1 for ordinary hydrogen up to over 250 for the actinide metals.

megawatt   A million watts. See 'Units'.

meltdown   A possible consequence of a **loss-of-coolant accident** in a nuclear reactor, with the core of the reactor becoming heated above its melting point and collapsing into an unsalvageable mess. It is a criterion of good reactor design that (a) meltdown should be impossible, and (b) that if it happens it should not lead to the formation of a critical mass of fissile fuel sufficient to sustain a chain reaction.

mendelevium   The element with atomic number $Z = 101$, symbol Md, one of the **actinide** metals.

mercury cell   A kind of electrical **storage cell.** Zinc oxide is present in the anode and (with potassium hydroxide) in the electrolyte; mercuric oxide makes up the cathode. The mercury cell has many technical advantages, but the mercury content makes it expensive and somewhat hazardous when discarded.

meson   Any of a large family of subnuclear particles which mediate the force that binds atomic nuclei together. The most common meson is the pion, a particle which in its free state has a mass of about one-sixth that of a nucleon and decays within a matter of a few nanoseconds.

methanation   The conversion of gases such as carbon monoxide and hydrogen, got usually from coal gasification, into methane. The reaction is

$$3H_2 + CO \rightarrow CH_4 + H_2O$$

and is the final step in methods of manufacturing **synthetic natural gas**.

methane   A hydrocarbon gas, CH_4, combustible with a calorific value of some $56\,MJ\,kg^{-1}$. **Natural gas** consists mostly of methane, but methane can also be obtained for example by processing coal (**synthetic natural gas**) or by the fermentation of biomass (see **biological energy**). NB $1m^3$ of methane $= 0.67\,kg$.

methanol   The modern term for methyl alcohol, CH_3OH. It is a clean liquid fuel with a calorific value of about $20\,MJ\,kg^{-1}$ and, like methane, it can be produced as a form of **biological energy**. Methanol is coming into use as an additive to gasoline (making **gasohol**) for fuelling automobiles, thereby conserving oil.

MHD   See **magnetohydrodynamics**.

microwaves   Electromagnetic radiation with frequency lying below that of the infra-red but above that of radio waves. The wavelength range is roughly from a millimetre up to a few centimetres. Microwaves are used in communications, and intense beams of them may be used to transfer energy as in microwave ovens. A possible future application may be in energy transfer from a solar power satellite.

moderator   In a nuclear fission reactor, a moderator is a substance used in the core to slow down neutrons from the high velocities at which they are released in fission to the lower 'thermal' velocity range in which they can readily be absorbed by the fissile fuel nuclei. Materials such as carbon and heavy water (D_2O) have been commonly used for this purpose.

mole   A quantity of any substance amounting to 6.022×10^{23} atoms or molecules of it. The mole is defined so that it corresponds very nearly to a mass (in grams) equal to the atomic mass number (A) or the molecular weight of the substance.

molten-salt breeder reactor   See MSBR.

momentum   A quantity usually given by the product of the mass and the velocity of a body, and measured (SI system) in newton-seconds. Like energy, momentum is a conserved quantity, and it is closely linked with energy by relativity theory.

motor spirit   Fuel, derived from oil, used in ordinary automobile engines. It is known as 'gasoline' in the USA, 'petrol' in the UK, and by other names elsewhere.

MSBR Molten-salt breeder reactor   A type of **nuclear reactor** in which a mixture of hot salts acts both as fuel and as coolant.

Mtce   Abbreviation for megatonnes of coal equivalent; see 'Units', Table C.

Mtoe   Abbreviation for megatonnes of oil equivalent; see 'Units', Table C.

muon catalysed fusion   A possible way of stimulating nuclear fusion between isotopes of hydrogen by using negatively-charged muons— particles similar to electrons but over 200 times heavier. In the same way as electrons bind hydrogen nuclei in pairs into molecules (H_2), so can muons; but the greater mass of the muon reduces the size of the molecule in proportion. So, the hydrogen nuclei can be held about 0.5 nm apart instead of 100 nm. When the nuclei are so close together, the chance of them fusing together is enormously enhanced. If muon catalysed fusion occurs in any particular molecule, the muon responsible is then released and can be used again in the same way with other nuclei.

This scheme offers the possibility of generating large amounts of energy without the excessively high temperatures that are initially needed for other methods. To put it into practice it is necessary to use hydrogen in the form of its heavy isotopes deuterium and tritium, since the most efficient energy generation is when deuterium and tritium fuse. The hydrogen would be in the form of a tiny **fuel pellet**, which would be preheated by laser or ion beams, and the muons would also be directed into the pellet in the form of a beam.

The high energy input to produce the muon beam, and the short lifetime of a muon (a few microseconds), will make muon catalysed fusion difficult to achieve. However, there is optimism that it could be a clean and efficient way of initiating nuclear fusion and so bringing the pellet to a high temperature at which conventional nuclear fusion would take over.

MW   Abbreviation for megawatt; see 'Units'.

National Environmental Policy Act (NEPA)   The law in the USA requiring detailed examination of the environmental impact of any new project. The NEPA has implications for the licensing of nuclear plant and also for other large-scale energy projects such as the strip mining of coal.

national grid   Term used, especially in the UK, for the nationwide network of electricity lines. The grid enables power to be transferred over large distances in quick response to variations in demand.

natural gas   Probably a fossil hydrocarbon like oil and coal, but there is a possibility that some is of purely geological origin and comes from deep within the earth. Natural gas is mainly methane (CH_4) with about 10 per cent of other, heavier, hydrocarbon gases such as ethane. It has a calorific value of some 55 MJ/kg, and is popular as a clean and convenient fuel.

Known world reserves of natural gas are probably in excess of 2,500 EJ (energy equivalent), but actual resources are likely to be very much higher. See also **fossil fuels**.

neptunium   The element (symbol Np) of atomic number $Z = 93$, one of the **actinide** metals.

neutrino   One of the fundamental types of particle in nature, the neutrino is a massless fundamental particle given off in certain types of radioactive decay process (see **beta-decay**). Since they interact only very weakly with ordinary matter, neutrinos have no practical impact on everyday life, although they are of great importance to astrophysics and cosmology. A high proportion of the total energy of the universe is contained in neutrino radiation.

neutron   A kind of nucleon, i.e. one of the building-blocks of atomic nuclei. The neutron has a mass of 1.8×10^{-30} kg or, in the conventional units, 939.57 MeV/c^2, and is about 1 fm in diameter. It is similar to the proton but is electrically neutral, hence the name, and can be understood as a compound of three particular kinds of quark.

Neutrons are uncommon in nature because they decay radioactively with a half-life of 11 minutes, yielding protons. Symbolically:

$$n \rightarrow p + e^- + \text{antineutrino}.$$

This is a form of beta-decay. The practical importance of neutrons comes from the fact that a neutron can stimulate a nucleus of a fissile substance such as plutonium to undergo fission, with a release of energy. Neutrons can also be absorbed by 'fertile' nuclei (e.g. thorium) to produce additional fissile material. Neutrons will also be absorbed by the metal lithium with the production of the fusion fuel tritium. In fission reactors, neutrons are both a product and a cause of fission, a fact underlying the **chain reaction** concept. However, to ensure proper reactor operation, the flux of neutrons has to be carefully controlled—by **moderators** which slow neutrons down, by absorbers which remove them from circulation and by **reflectors** with the effect of preventing neutron loss by turning them back into the reactor core. Neutrons are copiously given off by the cores of fission reactors and can be a radioactive hazard through neutron activation; on the other hand their application in fuel-breeding makes neutrons very precious in the sense that they can be used to multiply man's energy resources many times over through the use of thorium and the heavy form of uranium (^{238}U).

neutron activation   There are some common elements which can easily absorb neutrons and turn into radioactive isotopes. One example is the production of radioactive tritium from the heavy isotope of hydrogen. Another is the transmutation of gold into mercury, through the activation of an isotope of gold which decays subsequently into mercury. The formula for this is:

$$n + {}^{197}\text{Au} \rightarrow {}^{198}\text{Au} \rightarrow {}^{198}\text{Hg} + e^-.$$

The last step is a beta-decay with half-life 2.7 days.

nickel–iron cell   An electric storage cell with electrodes of nickel and iron oxide in a potassium hydroxide electrolyte.

nitrogen   The gas which accounts for almost 80 per cent by volume of the earth's atmosphere, and the element (symbol N) of atomic number $Z = 7$. Nitrogen can link weakly with oxygen to produce oxides such as nitrous oxide (N_2O) and nitrogen dioxide (NO_2). These oxides are often given off by automobile engines, etc., and are regarded as pollutants, but eventually they are broken down into nitrogen and oxygen again by the atmospheric chemical processes brought about by sunlight.

nobelium   The element of atomic number $Z = 102$ (symbol No), one of the **actinide** metals.

Noether's theorem   A theorem in physics, little known and less appreciated, which (in the case of energy) relates the conservation of energy to the invariance through time of physical laws. The theorem therefore reveals a deep connection between the nature of energy and the nature of time. To oversimplify, one could say that energy is conserved because time always runs at the same rate.

Non-Proliferation Treaty (NPT)   A treaty put into effect by the UN in 1970 and ratified by more than 100 nations. Its aim is to prevent nuclear weapons from being proliferated through the misuse of commercial nuclear energy systems. In return for the necessary safeguards, nations accepting the NPT are guaranteed access to peaceful nuclear technology.

non-renewable energy   The category of energy sources that are not replenished by nature and will therefore become exhausted in the foreseeable future. These sources include the fossil fuels, and uranium as it is presently used. Some fuels, such as wood, are in principle renewable but should perhaps be regarded as non-renewable at the present rate of exploitation.

North Sea   Submarine field of oil and gas accounting for most of the known reserves in Western Europe and equivalent to something like 100 EJ of energy. The greater part is divided roughly 2:1 between the UK and the Norwegian sectors, with smaller deposits in Danish, West German and Dutch waters.

nuclear battery   Another term for an **isotopic power generator**.

nuclear energy   It may be released in the interactions or decays of atomic nuclei or neutrons. It is rooted in the powerful forces which bind protons and neutrons into nuclei, and so can be many orders of magnitude more powerful than chemical energy. There are three main forms of nuclear energy, namely (1) **fission** energy, the basis of conventional **nuclear reactors**, (2) **fusion** energy, which underlies the power of the sun and may in the future be made use of in **fusion reactors**, and (3) the energy of **radioactivity**, which is the origin of geothermal power and also has been exploited in **isotopic power generators**.

nuclear fuel cycles   Any complete system for the utilisation of nuclear fuel is known as a **fuel cycle**. The importance of a fuel cycle lies in the fact that it will determine demand for primary nuclear fuels (uranium, thorium, lithium, etc.), the inventory of secondary nuclear fuels such as plutonium, and the **waste** materials which must ultimately be disposed of. In addition, fuel cycles are closely linked with requirements for uranium enrichment facilities, reprocessing, and the like.

This concept is best illustrated through a selection from the many nuclear fuel cycles which have been proposed; seven different ones are described below, some based on fission, some on fusion, and some on a combination of the two.

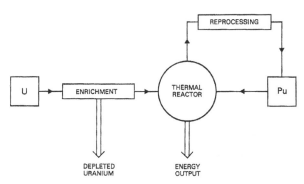

Figure 25 A thermal reactor fuel cycle. The primary input is uranium, and reprocessing permits some unburnt uranium together with produced plutonium to be recycled back in later fuel elements.

Figure 25 shows the thermal reactor cycle, fuelled primarily by enriched uranium, 'closed' by the reprocessing of the spent fuel so that the plutonium (Pu) formed in the reactor can be fed back in again as part of the fuel in new fuel elements. Although technically straightforward, this cycle has the disadvantages of requiring some trade in plutonium and of wasting the energy potential of the unused depleted uranium.

A cycle involving fast breeder reactors is shown in Figure 26. This could in principle use uranium very efficiently, but at the cost of

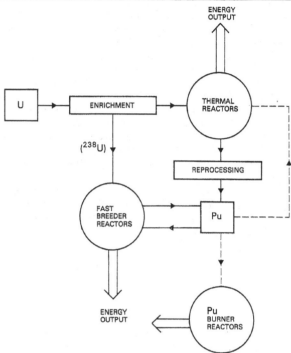

Figure 26 A fuel cycle using fast reactors. Plutonium, initially got from the reprocessing of thermal reactor fuel, is used to run breeder reactors which produce more plutonium from fertile ^{238}U; this plutonium can be used either in thermal reactors or in special plutonium burners.

handling large quantities of plutonium. Two or even three different reactor types need to be used.

Figure 27 illustrates the thorium cycle in its simplest form. A thermal reactor (which need not be dissimilar to many existing uranium reactors) is used both to consume the isotope ^{233}U and to 'breed' it from an input of thorium. But since thorium is not itself fissile, the cycle is not self-starting and any such reactor will need an initial input of fissile material from elsewhere. In fact, it is not clear that a good breeding ratio could ever be achieved with thorium alone; constant 'seeding' with other fissile material may be necessary.

In Figure 28 is shown a promising fuel cycle based on the fusion of deuterium and tritium, with the tritium 'bred' out of lithium with the neutron flux which would be given off by such a reactor.

96

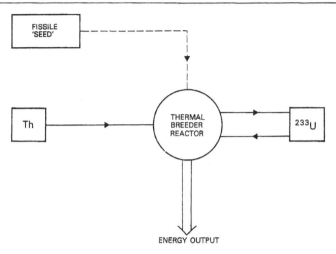

Figure 27 The thorium cycle. While thorium is the main input, the energy actually comes from the fission of uranium (^{233}U) which is being continuously 'bred' from the thorium.

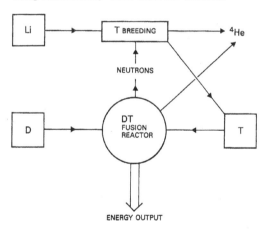

Figure 28 The lithium–tritium fuel cycle, in which a fusion reactor consumes deuterium (D) together with tritium (T), the latter being 'bred' out of lithium (Li) by the neutrons given off by the reactor. Apart from energy, the fusion product is ordinary helium (He).

A more sophisticated fusion fuel cycle, with two kinds of reactor, is illustrated in Figure 29. The DT/DD reactor would be a large and

97

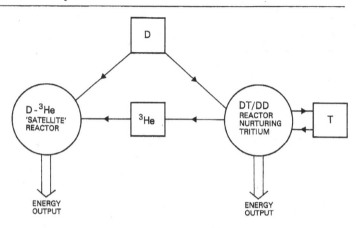

Figure 29 A more complex fusion fuel cycle.

technologically advanced one, with DT fusion creating temperatures adequate for DD fusion to take place. In these circumstances a certain amount of tritium would be produced (to be fed back in as fuel) and also the helium isotope ^{3}He could be collected: the ^{3}He could subsequently be used in relatively simple, small-scale 'satellite' reactors. The only net input is of deuterium.

Figure 30 shows a proposed fission–fusion hybrid fuel cycle. Fusion occurs in a deuterium-burning 'catalysed fusion' reactor, i.e. in which the tritium and helium (^{3}He) produced are immediately available for fusion in their turn, and by their higher energy release serve to catalyse the fusion of further deuterium. This is a complex and inefficient fusion reactor, actually requiring a net energy input, but it serves the purpose of generating a copious flux of neutrons. A blanket of uranium absorbs these neutrons with consequent plutonium production.

Finally, a 'symbiotic' system of fusion and fission reactors is shown in Figure 31. The fusion reactor is of the DT kind, the tritium being produced from lithium actually inside a molten-salt thermal fission reactor. The latter burns the uranium isotope ^{233}U bred from thorium in the blanket of the fusion reactor. The net inputs are thorium, lithium and deuterium, and no plutonium is involved.

It must be emphasised that all the above cycles have advantages and disadvantages which cannot be listed here, and that most, especially those involving fusion, are very far from being used in practice.

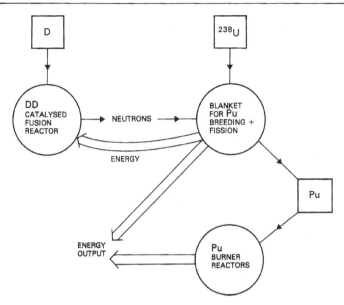

Figure 30 A hybrid fission–fusion fuel cycle. A fusion reactor fuelled only by deuterium (D), and requiring an energy input, produces neutrons which 'breed' plutonium and give some fission energy in a blanket surrounding the fusion reactor.

nuclear incineration The exposure of radioactive waste material to the intense neutron flux in a reactor core, bringing about the much more rapid decay of the material so that it will be safer in the long term. Nuclear incineration is particularly promising for dealing with long-lived **actinide** isotopes: by absorbing neutrons they can be converted into other isotopes which may decay more quickly, and although this implies higher activity in the short term it means that the risk of keeping material which is radioactive for tens of thousands of years may be avoided.

nuclear reactors Devices in which atomic nuclei are allowed to interact in a controlled way giving a yield of energy in the form of heat (see **nuclear energy**). It is possible that in the future **fusion reactors** will be built, but all existing commercial reactors are based on **fission**.

The only naturally-occurring fissile material is the uranium isotope ^{235}U, but natural uranium as mined contains only a small proportion of ^{235}U in comparison with a heavier isotope, ^{238}U. So, a process of enrichment is needed to produce uranium fuel for most

99

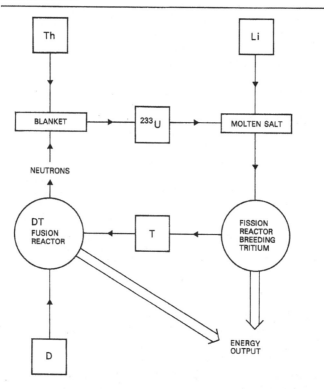

Figure 31 A symbiotic system of fission and fusion reactors.

reactors. However, as detailed below, there are other types of reactor which can be fuelled with natural uranium and others which
use **breeder** reactions to produce fissile material from thorium or
from the heavy uranium isotope ^{238}U. See **nuclear fuel cycles**.

Figure 32 illustrates some general features of reactor operation.
There is a core where the nuclear heat is generated, firmly contained
to avoid radiation outside it and (in case of accident) to prevent loss
of radioactive materials. A coolant fluid is pumped into the core,
circulates within it, and emerges at high temperature; the loop is
completed outside the core by a heat exchanger where steam is
raised. The core and the entire primary coolant loop are enclosed in
an outer containment vessel, which will also have within it a variety
of equipment for core control, refuelling, etc. In a separate building
the steam may be used to drive a turbine, giving mechanical power
with which electricity may be generated. Although the figure is

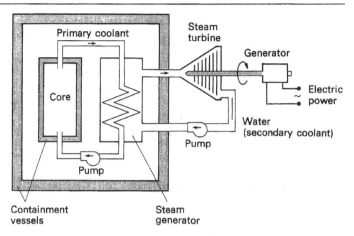

Figure 32 Layout of a nuclear power reactor.

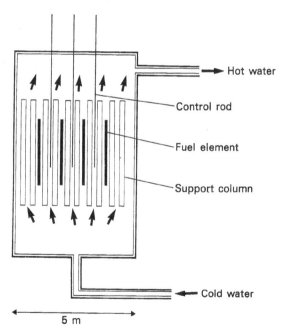

Figure 33 Schematic diagram of a PWR core.

101

drawn with a large central power plant in mind, the principle is the same for miniaturised reactors such as those used in submarine propulsion.

In practice, the majority of reactors are LWRs (light-water reactors) in which the primary coolant is ordinary water, H_2O). The LWRs fall into two sub-classes, BWRs (boiling-water reactors) and PWRs (pressurised water reactors). In the BWRs the core is designed in such a way that the coolant water boils within it: there is therefore no need for a separate steam generator, nor for a secondary coolant loop, features which make the design simple and convenient but make it difficult to ensure the same degree of safety as is found in other reactors. On the other hand, the popular PWRs have only liquid water in the core, with steam being raised in a secondary loop as in Figure 32. The primary coolant output temperature for a PWR is not much higher than for a BWR, but the pressure is about double in order to prevent boiling. The PWR core is illustrated schematically in Figure 33: the water flows through an array of parallel fuel elements and control rods, carrying off the heat generated in the fuel elements and at the same time acting as the **moderator** essential for bringing about the nuclear fission. The control rods are absorbers of neutrons which can be lowered to quench, or raised to enhance, the reaction.

A quite different kind of reactor core is shown in Figure 34. This is the CANDU (Canadian deuterium–uranium reactor) in which the

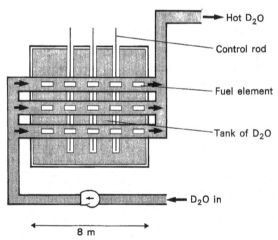

Figure 34 The CANDU reactor core.

102

primary coolant is **heavy water**, D_2O. This flows through the channels which contain the fuel elements, channels which are themselves contained in a tank of heavy water. The whole arrangement is known as a 'calandria'. The use of heavy water is prompted by its high effectiveness as a moderator, and in the CANDU design the neutron economy is good enough that natural uranium can be used as fuel instead of expensively enriched uranium.

A reactor's primary coolant need not be water, and there is an important family of reactors cooled by gases such as carbon dioxide and helium. It includes the MAGNOX reactors which have been working for many years in the UK. The choice of cladding alloy, the use of a graphite moderator, and carbon dioxide as coolant lead to a good neutron economy which permits the MAGNOX reactor, like the CANDU, to run on natural rather than enriched uranium. The successor to the MAGNOX is the AGR (advanced gas-cooled reactor) shown in Figure 35. It has many features in common with the MAGNOX, but burns slightly enriched uranium (2.3% ^{235}U) and provides higher-temperature steam so that a more efficient steam cycle can be used to generate electricity. The diagram, of course, gives only the principles of operation and the general layout: in fact

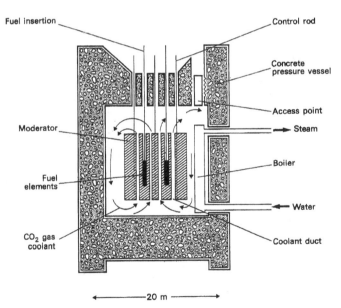

Figure 35 The layout of an AGR.

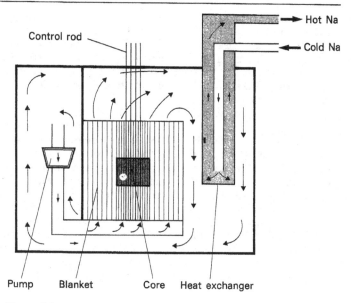

Figure 36 The LMFBR core.

there are no fewer than 332 fuel channels in the core, 89 control rods and 4 boiler units.

So far, only 'burner' reactors have been described, which generate heat by the fission of ^{235}U. A much wider range of designs opens up when breeder reactors are considered, capable of utilising ^{238}U or thorium, and the most advanced of these is the LMFBR (liquid-metal-cooled fast breeder reactor). It is a 'fast' reactor in the sense that the core contains fast, unmoderated, neutrons sufficient to breed a substantial amount of plutonium from ^{238}U. The fissile fuel in the core is itself plutonium, and there is a blanket region which initially contains no fissile material but the 'fertile' uranium isotope ^{238}U. In the blanket, and to some extent within the core as well, fresh plutonium is bred as the reactor runs, and can be recovered by the reprocessing of the fuel elements. The LMFBR is cooled by liquid sodium (Na) as shown in Figure 36, in both primary and secondary loops. A tertiary coolant loop outside the reactor vessel raises steam for electricity generation.

Another type of fast reactor is the GCFR (gas-cooled fast breeder reactor), which is cooled by helium gas rather than liquid sodium; it has the feature that thorium may be used as the 'fertile' material around the highly enriched uranium core, breeding fissile ^{233}U instead of plutonium.

Not all breeders are fast, and there are reactors with moderated slow neutrons in which fuel breeding can occur, although for the most part the fertile material must then be thorium. A particularly interesting example is the MSBR (molten-salt breeder reactor), shown schematically in Figure 37. The molten salt is a mixture of lithium, beryllium, thorium and uranium fluorides (68%, 20%, 12% and $\frac{1}{3}$% respectively), the uranium being the isotope ^{233}U 'bred' artificially from the thorium. The ^{233}U is the reactor's fissile fuel. The molten salt is continuously pumped out of the core and through a heat exchanger, but outside the core it does not form a critical mass and no fission occurs. Inside the core, the liquid is guided through a number of pipes close together so that there can be a critical mass, and a surrounding graphite moderator completes the trick. The MSBR has a secondary coolant circuit with a different hot salt, and would have a tertiary steam-raising circuit.

Other thermal breeder reactors include the **HTGR** (high-temperature gas-cooled reactor) and the **LWBR** (light-water breeder reactor), the latter being a variation on the PWR theme. Data on these, and on all the reactor types mentioned above, are summarised in Table 12.

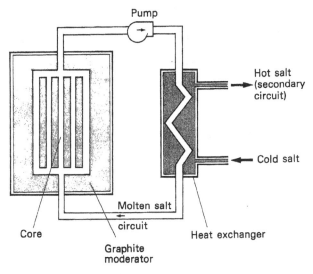

Figure 37 Schematic diagram of an MSBR core.

Table 12 *Nuclear fission reactor types**

Acronym	Fuel	Enrich-ment	Moder-ator	Primary coolant	Output temp. (C)	Eff. (%)
AGR	UO_2	2.3%	Graphite	CO_2	650	42
BWR	UO_2	2.6%	H_2O	H_2O	290	32
CANDU	UO_2	Natural	D_2O	D_2O	305	30
GCFR	UO_2 with ThO_2		None	He	550	36
HTGR	UO_2 with ThO_2		Graphite	He	1,370	39
HTR	UO_2	10%	Graphite	He	720	39
LMFBR	$PuO_2 + UO_2$	20% Pu	None	Na	620	44
LWBR	$ThO_2 + UO_2$	6% fiss.	H_2O	H_2O	320	32
MAGNOX	U	Natural	Graphite	CO_2	400	31
MSBR	Molten salt**		Graphite	(fuel)	705	~ 40?
PWR	UO_2	3.2%	H_2O	H_2O	320	32
SGHWR	UO_2	2.2%	D_2O	H_2O	270	32

*Much of these data, especially those on primary coolant output temperatures and steam cycle efficiencies, are not precise and will vary from one particular reactor to another.
**This mixture of hot molten salts also acts as the primary coolant.

The future development of nuclear reactors is a sensitive and controversial subject because of commercial rivalries, environmental concern and political worry over weapons proliferation. These factors are not independent but play upon one another in complex ways. However, there is a consensus of opinion that nuclear fission power is technically viable and can supply much of mankind's energy needs in the long term; the only real alternative is a dramatic expansion in the coal industry which could have an environmental impact no less harmful than that due to nuclear energy. But the problems of energy for the less-developed world, and of nuclear weapons proliferation, remain to be solved.

nuclear waste   High-level nuclear waste consists of the intensely radioactive used fuel elements and other material from nuclear reactor cores. Its radioactivity arises in part from fission products (e.g. ^{90}Sr and ^{131}I) which are short-lived but have special biological dangers, and in part from **actinides**, heavy metals of often very protracted radioactivity. Since used fuel elements contain a good deal of radioactive fissile material, including unconsumed fuel, **reprocessing** is likely to be an important part of any long-term nuclear waste disposal strategy.

Lower-level nuclear wastes will include all the lightly active objects from reactor environments—tools, soiled protective garments, etc., and even perhaps run-off rainwater—all of which need to be taken into account in assessing reactor safety. The importance of low-level waste is controversial: it can affect the population as a whole, not just workers in the nuclear industry, but it seems at present to be negligible compared with natural sources of radio-activity. On the other hand it will have to be controlled with increasing care if nuclear-power use expands in the future.

nucleon   Either a proton or a neutron. See **atom**.

nucleus   The dense, heavy core of an **atom**, inaccessible to chemical processes but mutable through the much more energetic nuclear reactions.

nuclide   The nucleus of a particular isotope of a particular element. Examples are the deuteron (^{2}H or D), the alpha-particle (^{4}He), fissile natural uranium (^{235}U) and indeed any combination of nucleons which may be found to exist.

Oak Ridge   Research centre and nuclear complex in Tennessee, USA, where research reactors, a gaseous diffusion plant and other facilities have been sited. In recent years the centre has diversified into a number of non-nuclear-energy research fields.

ocean–thermal energy conversion (OTEC)   A technique for extracting useful energy from the heat in the surface layers of ocean water which are warmed by the sun. OTEC systems are sometimes called 'SSPPs' or solar sea power plants. Such plants can generate electricity by exploiting the difference in temperature between the warm surface water and the colder water a few hundred feet below. The OTEC idea was pioneered by the French scientist Georges Claude over fifty years ago, but interest has recently been revived and a number of detailed designs have been put forward; one example is shown in Figure 38.

The OTEC system shown is a 'closed cycle' system using propane as the working fluid, boiled and cooled by the seawater but not mixed with it. (There are other 'open cycle' proposals which use the seawater itself as the working fluid.) Large quantities of surface water

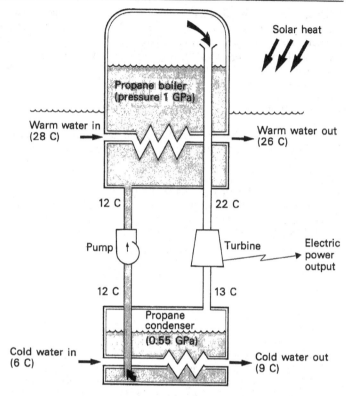

Figure 38 A solar sea power plant using a closed propane cycle.

pass through a boiler which vaporises the propane, the vapour drives an electricity-giving turbine and then is condensed by the cooling action of low-temperature deep water.

OTEC systems, to be effective, need to reach down through a considerable depth of water and so must be large and capital-intensive. No commercially successful device has yet been built.

octane A parameter used to measure the 'anti-knock' quality and therefore the efficiency of combustion of fuels for spark-ignition internal combustion engines. The octane number of a fuel is defined with reference to two reference fuels: namely iso-octane (octane number 100) and n-heptane (octane number 0).

oil   A liquid hydrocarbon refined from crude oil or, rather rarely, produced from coal, tar sands or oil shale. The term is often used loosely without distinction between crude and refined oil. See also **fossil fuels, fuels.**

oil shale   Shale, i.e. sedimentary rock, in which a wax-like hydrocarbon called kerogen is trapped. As a fossil-fuel resource oil shales are potentially very valuable, since the deposits existing are enormous. In the western USA, in Wyoming, Utah and Colorado, there may be a quantity equivalent to around 10^{12} barrels of oil in fairly rich shales (say, with more than 25 gallons of oil per tonne of shale), and very much more again where the proportion of hydrocarbon is lower. Other amounts are to be found in South America, and to a lesser degree in the other continents.

Shale oil recovery is not a proved technology, and it is not yet clear if it can become economically viable; in any case large-scale exploitation would have a severe environmental impact because of the high volumes of shale and overburden. On optimistic estimates it may be possible to extract economically as much as 100 million barrels of shale oil in the USA and maybe twice as much again elsewhere in the world.

OPEC   The Organisation of Petroleum Exporting Countries.

open-cast mining   The same as strip mining.

OTEC   Ocean-thermal energy conversion.

Otto cycle   The idealised **thermodynamic cycle,** which is the basis of the ordinary internal combustion engine. The cycle (see Figure 39) consists of (1) the isentropic compression of a fuel-air mixture, (2) the heating and sharp pressure rise resulting from combustion at constant volume, (3) an isentropic expansion giving mechanical power and (4) an exhaust of the gas to normal pressure.

An Otto cycle engine will convert heat to mechanical power with a theoretical maximum efficiency given by

$$\eta = 1 - r^{1-\gamma}$$

where r is the compression ratio, equal to V_b/V_a, and γ is a number (the ratio of specific heats) which for air is about 1.4. Since a typical compression ratio is about 10, it follows that the efficiency of such an engine cannot exceed 60 per cent or so.

oxyacetylene   See acetylene.

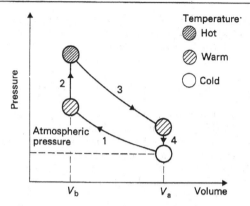

Figure 39 The Otto cycle, principle of the internal combustion engine.

oxygen The element of atomic number $Z = 8$, symbol O, abundant in the earth's crust and atmosphere. Over billions of years the oxygen in the atmosphere has built up through plant photosynthesis, and it can be looked on as an energy store now equivalent to about 2×10^{25} J. Of course this energy is not readily accessible, since fuels have to be found with which the oxygen may react.

paraffin (1) In the UK, the traditional name for **kerosine**, widely marketed in the past as a fuel for domestic heaters. (2) Waxy hydrocarbons (alkanes) familiar in the making of candles.

peat A soft fossil fuel, formed recently in geological terms and with a calorific value much lower even than that of wood. It is used in Ireland and in the USSR. See also **fuels**.

pebble-bed reactor A kind of nuclear fission reactor whose core consists of pebble-like balls of fuel and moderator, with a coolant gas passing up through the 'pebbles'.

Peltier effect See **thermoelectricity**.

petrol Colloquial name (in the UK) for petroleum-derived automobile fuel.

petroleum A general term for liquid fossil hydrocarbons. See also **oil**.

photon The fundamental quantum of electromagnetic radiation, i.e. the atom of light. The photon is massless but carries energy in proportion to the frequency of the radiation.

photosynthesis The conversion of carbon dioxide and water into carbohydrates and oxygen, carried out by green plants under the action of sunlight. Symbolically,

$$CO_2 + H_2O + sunlight \rightarrow CH_2O + O_2.$$

This reaction is catalysed by chlorophyll, and the **carbohydrates** made (CH_2O) form the bulk of plant material and include cellulose. Carbohydrates can be regarded as a stored form of the solar energy used in photosynthesis.

photovoltaic cell A device for converting the energy of **solar radiation** into electrical power. Photovoltaic cells are based on semiconducting materials, the most usual being **silicon**, although others such as gallium arsenide are occasionally used. Figure 40 shows schematically how a silicon cell operates. There is a piece of doped n-type silicon crystal with a surface layer of p-type silicon; between them a voltage exists because of the electronic properties of these forms of silicon, but it is a voltage that would not normally sustain a current or pro-

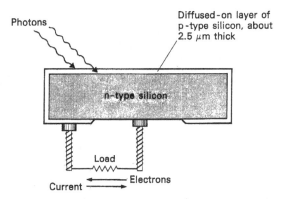

Figure 40 Schematic diagram of a photovoltaic cell.

vide energy. However, when light shines on the cell, photons are absorbed and release electrons from the crystal lattice; these electrons are drawn across the junction between the p-type and n-type crystals and so a current is made to flow.

Of the light from the sun, only about 44 per cent consists of sufficiently energetic photons to release electrons in the silicon, and of the resulting electric power no more than 50 per cent can be harnessed in an external load, so overall this type of cell cannot convert solar energy with more than 22 per cent efficiency. In practice it is usually even less, about 10 per cent.

The usefulness of photovoltaic cells arises from the fact that they use a free source of copious energy, namely the sun, but they have the disadvantage at the moment of high capital cost. In the future it may become possible to fabricate them in large quantities much more cheaply, in which case widespread domestic use and even photovoltaic central power stations could become a reality. See also **satellite solar power system**.

Planck's constant The universal constant which relates the energy of a quantum of radiation to its frequency or wavelength. The energy is

$$E = h\nu = hc/\lambda$$

where h is Planck's constant, 105×10^{-36} J s; ν is the frequency; c is the speed of light, 0.3 Gm s^{-1}; and λ is the wavelength.

plasma The state of a gas when it has been heated to such a temperature that molecules have become dissociated into atoms, and atoms have become ionised, by molecular and atomic collisions.

plutonium The element of atomic number $Z = 94$, symbol Pu, one of the **actinide** metals. Plutonium is not normally found in nature but it can be manufactured readily through the nuclear reactions occurring in uranium-fuelled reactors.

The lightest isotope is ^{238}Pu, which has a half-life of 88 years and a thermal power of 0.57 watt/gm and so is useful in isotopic power generators. The isotope ^{239}Pu is the one most copiously produced from uranium (see **breeder reactions**) and has a half-life of 24,400 years. ^{239}Pu is the form of plutonium used as a fuel in fast reactors and as a military nuclear explosive, but it must be remembered that in practice any sample of plutonium will contain more than one isotope: the isotopes are impossible to separate cleanly.

Heavier plutonium isotopes have mass numbers (A) from 240 to 244, the heaviest (^{244}Pu) being the most stable with a half-life of 83 million years. See also **nuclear fuel cycles**.

poisoning The reduction in efficiency of a nuclear fission reactor which will follow the production of neutron-absorbing fission products. The most important 'poisons' are isotopes of xenon (^{135}Xe) and samarium (^{149}Sm).

pollutant A by-product of any industrial, agricultural or energy-conversion process, released to the environment, which has an adverse effect. From energy conversion the pollutants of greatest concern have been the wastes associated with nuclear power, accidentally released crude oil and the oxides of carbon, sulphur and nitrogen given off in fossil-fuel burning.

polonium The element of atomic number $Z = 84$, symbol Po. None of its isotopes is stable and it occurs naturally only in minute amounts formed in the decay chains of natural uranium and thorium. One isotope, ^{210}Po, is used in isotopic power generators and is made from bismuth by the neutron activation of ^{209}Bi and the subsequent beta-decay of ^{210}Bi.

positron A subnuclear particle, the antiparticle of the **electron**, often given off in nuclear beta-decay.

potassium The element of atomic number $Z = 19$, symbol K. It is very abundant in the earth and one isotope, ^{40}K, is radioactive with a half-life exceeding a billion years. ^{40}K is responsible in part for the earth's internal heat manifested as geothermal energy.

potential energy Energy possessed by a body or system on account of work done against gravitational, electromagnetic or mechanical forces. It is to be contrasted with kinetic energy, or energy of motion. The energy in a storage cell, or in compressed air, can be regarded as potential energy; most commonly the term refers to gravitational potential energy, which under the earth's gravity is 9.8 J for every kilogram raised through a height of one metre. In terms of gravitational potential, the energy consumed by the average American would raise him by over 16 metres per second.

power For any system which produces, converts or consumes energy, the 'power' (in watts) is the rate (in joules per second) at which it does so. See also 'Units'.

power station Any large installation for the generation of electric power. The primary energy sources are usually fossil fuels, but nuclear energy and hydropower are becoming more and more important. Smaller power stations may also be based on solar or geothermal energy. See also **electricity**.

pressure   The measure of how strongly a force acts over a surface. Pressure is force per unit area, in SI units newtons per square metre or pascals (Pa).

The pressure of the atmosphere at sea level is 1.01325×10^5 Pa, sometimes called 1.01325 bar or 1013.25 millibars.

pressurised water reactor   See **PWR**.

primary electricity   Electric power generated from nuclear heat, tidal power, wind power, hydroelectric schemes and the like. It is so called because such sources cannot for the most part be exploited in any other way but through electricity. It is to be distinguished from secondary electricity got from the heat of combustion of fuels such as coal, and which represents one of many alternative uses for the fuel. The distinction is crucial in energy accounting because of the inefficiency of secondary electricity production.

primary energy   Primary energy sources, or primary fuels, are the forms in which energy occurs naturally before being converted into **secondary fuels** such as refined petroleum. See also **primary electricity**.

propane   A hydrocarbon (C_3H_8) obtained from crude oil and sometimes marketed in pressurised liquid form mixed with **butane**. Calorific value = 46 MJ/kg. See also **LPG**.

propanol (C_3H_8O) or propyl alcohol   A less common form of alcohol, with a calorific value of 32 MJ/kg.

propene (C_3H_6)   A hydrocarbon alkene with a calorific value of 46 MJ/kg.

propylene   The same as **propene**.

protactinium   The element of atomic number $Z = 91$, symbol Pa, one of the **actinide** metals.

proton   A kind of nucleon, i.e. one of the types of particle out of which all atomic nuclei are built up. A proton weighs 1.8×10^{-30} kg, is about 1 fm in diameter, and a single proton is the nucleus of the simplest element, hydrogen. Unlike the other kind of nucleon, the neutron, the proton carries an electric charge.

proved reserves   Resources of fossil fuels or minerals which, according to geological and other data, seem assuredly recoverable under present-day technical and economic conditions.

PS (abbr. for Pferdestaerke)   The same as **CV**.

pumped storage   A method of storing energy by pumping water up a gradient from a low to a high reservoir. Later, when needed, the energy can be converted back into electricity by passing it down again through generating turbines.

Pumped storage systems can be easily incorporated in many hydroelectric or tidal-power schemes and for following a fluctuating electricity demand they can be more economical than nuclear or fossil-fuel-fired plant.

purex (acronym for Plutonium and Uranium Recovery by EXtraction). A process commonly used to separate out the eponymous actinides from used reactor fuel. See also **reprocessing**.

Putnam   The Putnam wind turbine is a horizontal-axis aerogenerator. It is a large machine, with a two-bladed rotor sweeping around every second or so.

PWR   Pressurised water reactor. A nuclear fission reactor cooled by ordinary water kept from boiling by containment under high pressure. See also **nuclear reactors**.

pyrolysis   Treatment with heat. For example, if a hot gas (at, say, 800 C) is passed through a subterranean deposit of coal, light hydrocarbons may be driven off and recovered; this may be the most economical way of exploiting some low-grade coal deposits. Another example of pyrolysis is the proposed heat-treatment of domestic refuse to yield a convenient combustible fuel.

Q   A large unit of energy, equal to 1,000 quads, i.e. to 1,055 EJ. See also 'Units', Table B.

quad (abbr. q)   A unit of energy equal to 10^{15} Btu, i.e. to 1,055 EJ. See also 'Units', Table B.

quark   While atomic nuclei consist of nucleons, nucleons in their turn are composed of still more elementary entities known as quarks. There are for most purposes three quarks in a nucleon, and two kinds of quark (the 'up' quark u and the 'down' quark d) readily occur in nature. The two common nucleons have the compositions

proton p   = u + u + d
neutron n   = u + d + d

and nuclear beta-decay arises from transitions (involving electron emission) between u and d quarks.

Q-value   (1) In a nuclear decay, the total energy which appears as kinetic energy and eventually as heat is the 'Q-value' and is proportional to the mass of the decaying particle less the masses of the decay products. (The constant of proportionality is the square of the velocity of light, c.)

(2) When an energy-storing system is oscillating or rotating in some way (e.g. a flywheel) and thereby dissipates some of its energy, the 'Q-value' is the number 4π divided by the fractional energy loss per cycle. If the flywheel loses 1 per cent of its energy at each revolution, Q = 1,257. The higher the Q-value, the better the system.

rad (abbr. for radiation absorbed dose)   The unit by which doses of **radiation** are measured. One rad is defined as the dose under which 10 millijoules of energy will be deposited in each kilogram of exposed material.

A new standard unit, the **gray**, is now coming into use and is equal to 100 rad. Moreover there is a further unit, the **rem**, which measures more closely the biological effect of a radiation dose.

radiation   A term that covers electromagnetic radiation such as the light from the sun, the ionising radiation associated with nuclear reactions and other, less relevant, emanations such as gravitational radiation.

Ionising radiation is usually given off by **radioactive** substances, and it can be subdivided into **alpha-, beta-** and **gamma-radiation**. The flux of **neutrons** from a reactor core is also a form of radiation. Exposure to radiation is measured by units such as the **roentgen**, the **gray**, the **rad** and the **rem**, the latter being the most useful for quantifying the health effect of radiation from the environment.

Table 13 *Average radiation doses to the general population from various sources**

Source	Dose (mrem/year)
Natural	
Cosmic rays	45
The earth	60
^{40}K in the body	17
^{14}C in the body	1
Ra, etc., in the body	7
Artificial	
Medical sources	76
Weapons fallout	4
Miscellaneous	3
Total	213

* The radiation dose from nuclear power to the average person is well below 1 mrem/year and so does not appear in the table.

Table 13 indicates the doses in mrem/year to which the average person is exposed. For those with an occupational risk of exposure to radiation, there are recommended maximum doses varying from one organ of the body to another, but typically an order of magnitude below the normal average background dose.

radioactivity The phenomenon by which energy, in the form of radiation and heat, is given off through the nuclear decay of certain substances.

According to the nature of the radiation, radioactivity can be classified into **alpha-, beta-** and **gamma-activity**. All atomic nuclei which are not absolutely stable are radioactive, and in fact this applies to the great majority of the nuclei which have been discovered. For example the element thorium has eight known isotopes, of which four (^{227}Th, ^{228}Th, ^{229}Th and ^{230}Th) are alpha-active, three (^{231}Th, ^{233}Th and ^{234}Th) are beta-active and one (^{232}Th) is almost stable; but even this latter is very slightly radioactive, decaying with a **half-life** of 14 thousand million years. Moreover, all eight isotopes emit gamma-rays along with their alpha- or beta-rays.

Dangerously radioactive materials tend, by their very nature, to decay away quickly; since the earth is so ancient, few radioactive materials occur within it nowadays. Of those that do, the most note-worthy are isotopes of potassium (^{40}K), thorium (^{232}Th) and ura-nium (^{235}U and ^{238}U). See also **geothermal energy.**

radioisotope   Any isotope of any element which is radioactive.

radium   The element of atomic number $Z = 88$, symbol Ra. One of its isotopes (^{226}Ra) is an important decay product of uranium (^{238}U) and can be separated out from uranium ore.

radon   The element of atomic number $Z = 86$, symbol Rn. Like radium, it is a product of uranium, but radon is more highly radio-active and, as a gas, can be hazardous to those mining or processing uranium ore.

rail   A common transport method traditionally powered by coal-burning steam-engines but which now more often uses diesel engines or electricity. See also **transport.**

Rance   A river in Brittany, opening into the sea by St Malo, whose estuary has been used for a pioneering tidal-power scheme rated at 240 MW.

Rankine cycle   A thermodynamic cycle which is the principle under-

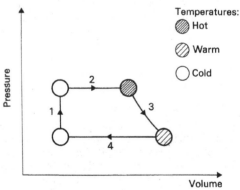

Figure 41 The Rankine (steam) cycle.

lying the steam turbine. Figure 41 illustrates the steps in terms of the pressure and volume of a quantity of water going through the cycle. We have (1) the increase in pressure as water is pumped in, (2) constant-pressure heat input raising steam, (3) the isentropic expansion of the steam, generating mechanical power, and to complete the cycle, (4) the condensation of the steam as it gives up its remaining heat at atmospheric pressure.

Rankine scale A temperature scale beginning at absolute zero but with Fahrenheit-sized degrees, so that the Rankine temperature is 1.8 times the Kelvin temperature.

reactivity In a nuclear fission reactor core, the reactivity is a measure of how rapidly the fission chain reaction is building up. It is given by

$$\rho = (k-1)/k$$

where k is the multiplication factor by which the neutron number is multiplied from one generation to the next of the chain reaction.

reactor See nuclear reactors.

refining The treatment of crude oil to produce particular hydrocarbon 'petroleum fractions' for use as fuels, lubricants and other purposes. Depending on the nature of the crude oil and the choice of products to be made, there are different steps that may make up the refining process. As a rule, it will be necessary to remove the non-hydrocarbon part of the crude oil, especially sulphur compounds. By distillation, light components can be separated off from heavier ones. There are 'cracking' techniques for breaking down heavy molecules, and methods such as alkylation or polymerisation to do the reverse. Finally, there will be a blending of hydrocarbons to give the wanted product, possibly with an admixture of some other quite different chemicals such as the lead compounds often added to automobile fuel.

reflectivity For any surface, the reflectivity is the proportion of light energy incident which will be immediately reflected back from it. The term is usually applied to visible light, in which case white objects and mirrors obviously have high reflectivity, but in general it depends on the wavelength of the radiation and the concept can be applied to radiant heat. The reflectivity differs from unity by an amount equal to the **absorptivity**; for typical values, see **emissivity**, Table 5.

119

reflector   In a nuclear reactor, a reflector is a substance used to surround the core with the aim of knocking back neutrons which emerge from it. Good reflectors are made from elements such as carbon that have nuclei which are light and which do not readily absorb neutrons.

refrigerants   Substances used in vapour compression cycle refrigerators and selected for the convenience of their boiling points and high latent heats. In practice freons or other halocarbons are used, and some typical parameters are listed in Table 14.

Table 14 *Some common refrigerants*

Formula	Standard number	Boiling point	Latent heat
CCl_3F	11	24 C	180 kJ/kg
CCl_2F_2	12	−30 C	165 kJ/kg
$CHClF_2$	22	−41 C	235 kJ/kg
$(CClF_2)_2$	114	4 C	135 kJ/kg
H_2O	718	100 C	2260 kJ/kg

refrigerator   A device for cooling an enclosed space, based on a **heat pump** cycle such as the **vapour compression cycle** or the **absorption cycle**. In the past, refrigerators have not usually been designed for efficiency or economy of use; but the present emphasis on conservation is leading to designs with better insulation, more efficient heat exchangers, smaller motors, etc.

rem (roentgen equivalent man)   The rem is the accepted unit of biologically effective **radiation** dose. It is very similar to the **rad**, but includes a 'quality factor' to account for the fact that some types of radiation are biologically more damaging than others even when the same amounts of energy are involved. That is to say,

rems = rads × quality factor

and recommended standard quality factors are listed in Table 15 for the different types of radiation.

renewable energy   A term used to cover those primary energy sources which, for practical purposes, can be considered inexhaustible. Renewable energy includes solar power, wind, wave and tide, and hydroelectricity. Geothermal energy and some forms of nuclear power may also be regarded as renewable.

Table 15 *Radiation quality factors (rems per rad)*

Radiation	Quality factor
X-rays	1
gamma-rays	1
beta-rays	
above 30 keV	1
below 30 keV	1.7
neutrons	
above 100 keV	11
intermediate	10
below 1 keV	2
alpha-rays	10
heavier nuclei	20

reprocessing   The treatment of used nuclear fuel elements so as to extract the remaining uranium and plutonium and to concentrate the radioactive waste for disposal. In the past there have been reprocessing schemes used for military purposes to extract plutonium from reactors designed to 'breed' it; currently, work is under way on reprocessing plants that will handle used uranium oxide fuel from commercial thermal reactors. Reprocessing is seen as necessary for three reasons: first, so as to make the most efficient use of uranium in existing reactors; second, so as to end the present unsatisfactory practice of storing untreated waste in bulk; third, so as to advance the technology which will be needed in the future for any large-scale use of commercial breeder reactors. See **nuclear fuel cycle**.

The first step in the reprocessing chain is an initial period of storage of the spent fuel under water for a time sufficient for the decay of the most highly active, heat-producing, isotopes in it. Subsequently the fuel elements will be taken apart and cut into small pieces which are put into nitric acid. The acid dissolves all but the metallic 'cladding' (of steel or zircaloy, for example), which is rinsed and removed as waste.

The next steps involve chemical treatment of the acid solution in which the fuel itself has been dissolved. The fission products can be separated out as high-level waste, and the uranium and plutonium also isolated.

Finally, the uranium that has been recovered will be sent for enrichment to be used again along with freshly-mined uranium; the plutonium will be blended in with uranium in new fuel elements.

reversibility A thermodynamic concept used especially in the context of stages in heat engine cycles. In simple terms, a reversible change to a system is one which can be 'run backwards' without any overall change to the system, such as a net loss of energy.

roentgen (abbr. R) The unit of exposure to **radiation**. It is defined in a rather cumbersome way as the amount of radiation which will ionise air to the extent of releasing electrons of total charge 2.58×10^{-4} coulombs per kilogram of air. This amounts roughly to the release of one in every 200 billion of the electrons in the air.

An exposure of 1 R in air corresponds approximately to an absorbed dose in the body of 0.96 **rad**.

Salter's duck A type of device for converting wave energy into a usable form. See also **wave energy**.

satellite solar power system (SSPS) A proposed method for exploiting solar energy on a large scale through orbiting arrays of solar cells. To be economically and energetically efficient, the scheme will need cheap and efficient silicon cells, re-usable spacecraft able to ship heavy loads into orbit and other prerequisites. Because of the size of the solar cell array, the satellite would require a substantial framework of metal girders, probably aluminium, and their energy intensiveness will be a key parameter to the overall system efficiency.

A typical design for an SSPS envisages an orbiting array of cells extending over 80 km² and producing some 8 GW of power. The electrical power would be converted into microwaves and transmitted down to the earth from a transmitting antenna about 1 km in diameter. On the ground, the power would be picked up by a 'rectenna' array extending over perhaps as much as 300 km² (but not denying that land to agricultural use). There seems to be no insuperable safety hazard or technical difficulty, but it is thought unlikely that SSPSs of this type could be in routine use within fifty years.

Savonius rotor A form of rotor for a **wind energy** machine, illustrated (Figure 42) in its vertical-axis 'split oildrum' version.

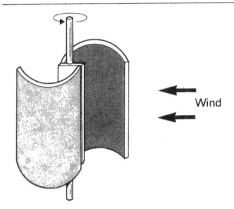

Figure 42 A simple Savonius rotor.

second law   The second law of **thermodynamics**, which may be stated as that no process is possible whose sole result is the complete conversion of heat into work.

secondary fuels   Fuels derived from natural, 'primary', sources of energy. While the primary fuels include raw coal, uranium, crude oil, sunshine and natural gas, the secondary fuels include refined fossil fuel products, electricity and sometimes heat itself. The distinction between primary and secondary fuels is important in energy economics; primary fuels are normally useless to final consumers of energy, while a secondary fuel will in general be deriveable from a range of primary fuels. See also **primary electricity**.

Seebeck effect   See **thermoelectricity**.

separative work   A term used in uranium enrichment. If an enrichment plant converts a mass F of input 'feed' into a mass P of product and W of waste, with enrichments x_f, x_p and x_w respectively, then the separative work is given by the formula

$$SW = W \cdot V(x_w) + P \cdot V(x_p) - F \cdot V(x_f)$$

where $V(x) = (2x - 1) \cdot \ln(x/(1 - x))$

Units of separative work, or 'separative work units' (SWU), can be given a cash value that reflects the economy of the enrichment plant.

Severn estuary   See **tidal energy**.

123

SGHWR   Steam-generating heavy water reactor. See **nuclear reactors**.

shale oil   Oil contained in, or extracted from, **oil shale**.

SI   Système International. Refers to the agreed conventions for the measurement of physical quantities. See 'Units'.

silicon   The element of atomic number $Z = 14$, symbol Si. It occurs naturally with great abundance. In its pure crystal form, silicon is a semiconductor of value in **photovoltaic cells**.

slurry   Coal slurry is a mixture of crushed coal with water, and in this form coal may be conveniently transported by pipeline over long distances. Typically, a slurry will consist of one part coal to three or four parts water, and can be pumped at about 5 metres per second. The technique is well established in many countries, but may be used on a much larger scale in the future to transport coal from the remote coalfields of the US Mid-West and of Siberia.

SNG   See **synthetic natural gas**.

sodium   The element of atomic number $Z = 11$, symbol Na. In the energy context it has important applications in nuclear engineering, where liquid sodium can be a useful core coolant, and in the sodium-sulphur cell.

sodium–sulphur cell   A kind of electrical **storage cell**, with the advantage of high energy density which makes it attractive for powering electric motors in vehicles. The main disadvantage of the sodium-sulphur (Na–S) cell is that it requires a high temperature for operation: it needs to be at about 300 C, well above the melting point of sulphur.

solar cell   A device for converting the energy of solar radiation directly into electricity. See also **photovoltaic cell**.

solar constant   The 'solar constant' is 1.353 kW m^{-2}, and is within 1 or 2 per cent of the total power that falls on an area directly facing the sun at the average sun-to-earth distance. The number given above is a standard value widely adopted for consistency of calculation, but in fact the power from the sun will vary somewhat according to the time of year and the conditions on the sun itself. Note that the solar constant refers to the radiation in space, not on the earth's surface. See also **solar radiation**.

solar energy   The energy given off by the sun in the form of electro-magnetic radiation, at a total rate of 380×10^{24} W. Of this, 173×10^{15} W, i.e. 0.173 EW, falls on the earth. The term 'solar energy' may be applied to any of the numerous ways in which this energy flow may be converted and utilised: as biological energy, wind energy, wave energy, ocean thermal energy, and especially as direct heat (see **domestic energy**) and **photovoltaic** energy. Solar energy has the advantage of being a constant, ever-renewed flow, but against this must in practice be weighed its variability and low average intensity. See also **solar radiation**.

solar furnace   An arrangement of mirrors to focus sunlight from a wide area onto a small volume. The radius of the earth's orbit is over 200 times the radius of the sun, so if the sunlight on a 2-metre square is concentrated onto 1 square centimetre there is a chance of reaching the temperature of the sun's surface.

In fact remarkably high temperatures, in the thousands of degrees, can be reached and sustained with solar furnaces, and they have been valuable research tools for studying the high-temperature properties of materials. Also, such a furnace can be used to raise steam to generate electricity, and small-scale power plants to do this have been built.

solar panel   See **flat-plate collector**.

solar radiation   Energy from the sun has an intensity of about 1353 W m^{-2} at the position of the earth's orbit: that is the rate at which energy flows through every square metre of area directly facing the sun. Of that which strikes the earth, a good deal is absorbed by the atmosphere even when the sky is clear, some 900 W m^{-2} reaching the surface when the sun is directly overhead. This is reduced further when the sun is lower, falling exponentially with increasing **air mass**. At any particular location the solar radiation at the surface obviously fluctuates; a rough average value for temperate latitudes is 100 W m^{-2}, averaged over all times and seasons.

The spectrum of the solar radiation is illustrated by Figure 43. This is how the energy is distributed across the range of wavelengths, and it can be seen that the spectrum attenuated by the atmosphere (lower curve) is not cut down uniformly but has some wavelengths for which atmospheric absorption is especially heavy; in fact for some wavelengths practically no radiation reaches the surface of the earth at all. In particular, the ultra-violet (UV) region at the left is soaked up by gases such as ozone in the upper atmosphere, while the infra-red (IR) region is heavily attenuated by carbon dioxide.

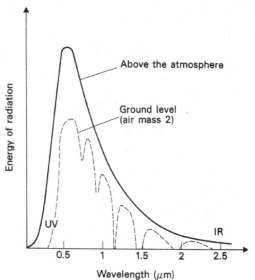

Figure 43 The solar radiation spectrum.

Another absorber is water vapour, responsible for some of the dips in the middle of the lower spectrum. See also **sun, atmosphere, solar energy**.

solar sea power plants (SSPP)   See **ocean–thermal energy conversion**.

space heating   The heating of the indoor environments in which people live and work. For comfort, the air within a building must be at a suitable temperature, and so must the inner wall surfaces. See also **domestic energy**.

spark ignition engine   An **internal combustion engine** which, unlike the diesel engine, uses an electric spark to ignite the fuel in the combustion chamber. The spark ignition engine is the most common kind of automobile engine. See also **transport**.

specific heat   See **heat capacity**.

SSPP   Solar sea power plants. See **ocean–thermal energy conversion**.

SSPS   Satellite solar power system.

steam The gaseous form of water, formed under atmospheric pressure at a temperature of 100 C. The transition from liquid to gas then requires an energy input (latent heat) of 2.26 MJ/kg.

Steam engines, which dominated the industrial revolution of the nineteenth century, are reciprocating engines with pistons powered by steam pressure. They are now virtually obsolete, and should not be confused with steam turbines. The latter are used very widely for generating electricity from steam raised by fossil-fuel combustion or by nuclear plants, and their principle of operation is the **Rankine cycle**.

Stefan–Boltzmann law This is the law that a body will radiate heat in proportion to the fourth power of its absolute temperature. To be exact, the power radiated per unit area is given by

$$\text{watts per square metre} = \epsilon \cdot \sigma \cdot T^4$$

where σ is the Stefan–Boltzmann constant and is equal to 5.67×10^{-8} in units of $W\,m^{-2}\,K^{-4}$. The factor ϵ is an average **emissivity** which depends on the nature of the surface and may vary somewhat with temperature. As a rule ϵ is not much below unity, and it is equal to unity in the ideal case of a perfectly emitting **black body**.

stellarator A type of toroidal magnetic confinement device for a plasma such as might be used for sustaining nuclear fusion.

Stirling engine A kind of external combustion engine which is illustrated schematically in Figure 44. A cylinder contains a gas which a displacer piston separates between a hot space and a cold space. When the displacer moves to the left the gas moves round, giving up heat to a regenerator (a porous material through which the gas is forced) and also losing heat to the surroundings through a **heat exchanger**. When the displacer moves to the right the gas goes back into the hot space, picking up heat from the regenerator and also from a heat exchanger to which energy is input by the combustion of a fuel externally.

To get mechanical power from the Stirling engine, a second piston compresses the gas when it is in the cold space and then (moving with the displacer) lets it expand when it is in the hot space. Naturally, a real engine is much more complex than the diagram would suggest, and the pistons move in a precise time sequence.

In recent years the Stirling engine has been examined as a possible alternative to traditional internal combustion engines, but has not been taken up on a large scale.

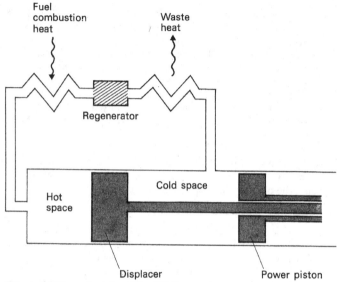

Figure 44 The principle of the Stirling engine.

stoichiometric When a fuel is burned, a certain amount of oxygen is taken in: the ratio of oxygen to fuel is stoichiometric when there is just enough oxygen for complete combustion but not more than is necessary. In general, the term is used for any chemical process when the ingredients are exactly balanced in quantity.

storage cell A kind of chemical energy store which will give its power in the form of an electric current. Other terms used are 'electric cell' (embracing also **fuel cell**), 'battery' (strictly, a set of several cells) and 'accumulator' (strictly, a rechargeable storage cell), but these terms are often applied loosely and interchangeably. A storage cell consists of two electrodes separated by a substance known as the 'electrolyte'. The electrodes are of different materials with different electrochemical potentials so that a voltage will be sustained between them: the electrodes often give their names to the cell, e.g. 'sodium–sulphur cell'. The electrolyte is chosen to permit a flow of chemical ions between the electrodes, and so an electric current, when the electrodes are linked through an external circuit. Electrolytes are acidic or alkaline, usually liquids or pastes.

A distinction is made between primary cells and secondary cells: the former must be thrown away (or, at best, recycled) when their power is exhausted, but secondary cells are rechargeable with an input current from an external source. For applications involving high power, and especially electric vehicles, rechargeability quick and often is essential.

An enormous number of types of storage cell can be made, but a few particular types have become widespread because of features such as cheapness, long life and compactness as well as rechargeability. Almost all cells supply between 1 and 2 volts, but by putting them in series higher voltages can readily be obtained. Energy densities vary widely according to design, lying usually between 50 and 300 kilojoules per kilogram (cf. 50 megajoules per kilogram for gasoline). However, new kinds of cell are under development which will permit still higher energy densities, e.g. the **sodium–sulphur** and **lithium–fluorine** cells.

Cells in common use include primary cells such as the **Leclanché cell** and the **Daniell cell**. Of secondary cells the best known is certainly the lead-acid cell, used universally for automobile engine starting and containing about 100 kJ/kg. Also of interest are 'air batteries', of which one electrode is actually given by the air (actually, oxygen); the zinc–air cell is an example.

stratified-charge engine A kind of internal combustion engine in which the fuel is not mixed homogeneously with air before ignition. Instead, there is a rich mixture to aid ignition surrounded by a weaker mixture which burns later. In some designs the combustion chamber is divided into two connected parts.

strip mining Sometimes called 'open-cast' mining: this is the mining of coal or other minerals from deposits very close to the surface by completely stripping away the material lying above the coal. Strip mining avoids the need for underground working, but its environmental impact is overwhelming. Strip mining is the necessary method of exploiting the vast shallow coal deposits in the midwestern USA and in Siberia.

strontium An element ($Z = 38$, symbol Sr) which is a nuclear fission product and, in its isotope ^{90}Sr, is radioactive with a half-life of 28½ years. ^{90}Sr is the major form of artificial global radioactivity arising from weapons testing and it could in principle be released through the mishandling of **nuclear waste**.

substitute natural gas The same as **synthetic natural gas**, a fuel consisting almost entirely of methane.

sun   The sun is a source of energy driven by thermonuclear fusion reactions deep in its core. This energy rises to the surface of the sun where the 'photosphere', at a temperature of approximately 5,760 K, radiates it away with a power of 3.8×10^{26} W.

The sun's output varies a little according to solar climatic phenomena such as the eleven-year sunspot cycle. See also **solar radiation**.

superconductivity   The phenomenon whereby many electrical conductors lose their resistance to a current when their temperatures are sufficiently low. It then becomes possible to maintain a very high electrical current in a thin conductor without appreciable energy loss.

The temperatures needed are typically in the 10–20 K region, depending on the material, and so **cryogenic** technology is required. This is well worth while in applications such as magnet coils for plasma confinement systems.

syncrude   A mixture of liquid hydrocarbons obtained from bitumen or tar, especially by a particular method developed by the Syncrude Co. of Canada. The method is being used to exploit the extensive tar-sands deposits in Alberta.

synthetic natural gas (SNG)   A fuel consisting mainly of methane and therefore interchangeable with natural gas. It is produced sometimes from light oil products (propane, butane, naphtha, etc.) and sometimes from coal through gasification and methanation.

tailings   The residue of uranium ore after it has been processed for the extraction of the uranium-rich **yellowcake**. When a tonne of yellowcake is produced there will be perhaps a hundred tonnes of tailings, useless and slightly radioactive.

tails   The residue of uranium enrichment, i.e. uranium depleted in the fissile isotope. Natural uranium contains only 0.7 per cent of the fissile isotope, the rest being the heavier isotope ^{238}U. If, for example, enriched uranium is produced with 5% fissile ^{235}U, and 10 kg of natural uranium are used up in giving 1 kg of enriched uranium, then the 9 kg of tails will have a 'tails assay' (i.e. ^{235}U fraction) equal to about 0.2 per cent.

tar Black, viscous liquid hydrocarbons, intermediate between oil and bitumen. Tar occurs naturally in its own right, e.g. in tar sands; it can be produced out of **coal** (coal tar) or as a residue from **crude oil**.

tar sands Deposits of sand or limestone containing oil. There are large quantities in Canada (the Athabasca tar sands, Alberta), the USA (Utah), Venezuela and other countries such as China. The cost of recovery can be high since a large mass of material has to be strip mined, perhaps nine-tenths of which is sand; the oil is extracted by pyrolysis.

Total tar-sands resources are very large, of the order of 10^{12} bbl or 10,000 EJ, but only a small proportion will be recoverable at reasonable cost. The economic limitation on tar sands may well be the fact that at a certain price liquid hydrocarbons can be manufactured from coal, which is far more abundant. See also **fuels**.

temperature The degree to which any substance contains heat energy, i.e. microscopic energy of atomic and molecular motion. If E is the average atomic or molecular kinetic energy, then the temperature is roughly E/k, where k is the Boltzmann constant, equal to 1.3807×10^{-23} J K^{-1}. This gives the **absolute** temperature, in degrees Kelvin (K), but the usual everyday scale is the **Celsius**, which has the same size of degree as the Kelvin scale but has its zero at the melting point of ice. The **Fahrenheit** scale is also still common.

In more precise **thermodynamic** terms, temperature is characterised by its transitivity, i.e. the fact that two bodies in equilibrium contact will be at the same temperature. Any difference in temperature implies a flow of heat from the warmer to the cooler body.

tetra-ethyl lead (TEL) A compound added to motor fuel at a concentration of rather less than 0.1 per cent in order to provide antiknock properties. TEL's chemical form is $Pb(C_2H_5)_4$.

tetra-methyl lead (TML) A compound similar in purpose to TEL, but with the structure $Pb(CH_3)_4$.

therm A unit of energy equal to 100,000 Btu and to 105.5 MJ. See 'Units', Table B.

thermal conductivity The readiness with which a substance will conduct heat. See also **conductivity**.

thermal neutron   A neutron in a fission reactor core with kinetic energy similar to that of the molecules of which the core is made. Neutrons are produced initially at much higher energies in the fission process but are slowed down ('moderated') by repeated collision until they are 'thermalised' at energies well below an electron volt.

thermal pollution   The discharge of waste heat to the environment. It is of most concern when large power stations release low-grade heat in water which can upset the ecologies of the rivers, estuaries or coastal waters where it is discharged.

thermal reactor   A kind of **nuclear reactor**, which has thermal neutrons within its core and produces energy mainly by the stimulated fission of ^{235}U. Practically all commercial nuclear reactors are thermal reactors, and are distinguished from 'fast' reactors which use higher-energy neutrons to breed plutonium.

thermie   A million calories. See 'Units', Table B.

thermocouple   An instrument for measuring temperature through the Seebeck effect, i.e. using the voltage which can appear between two junctions in an electrical circuit when they are at different temperatures. See also **thermoelectricity**.

thermodynamic cycles   In the analysis of the various kinds of heat engines it is often useful to consider idealised working cycles in which each step is perfectly isentropic, isobaric, isothermal or isovolumetric; this simply means that during each part of the cycle some parameter (entropy, pressure, temperature or volume) is kept constant. This leads to a family of thermodynamic cycles, and in particular the **Brayton, Carnot, Diesel, Otto** and **Rankine** cycles. Each cycle has four stages, as shown in Table 16. The main difference between the Rankine cycle and the Brayton cycle is that the former

Table 16 *Thermodynamic cycles*

Name of cycle	Stage			
	Compression	Heating	Expansion	Exhaust
Brayton	Isentropic	Isobaric	Isentropic	Isobaric
Carnot	Isentropic	Isothermal	Isentropic	Isothermal
Diesel	Isentropic	Isobaric	Isentropic	Isovol.
Otto	Isentropic	Isovol.	Isentropic	Isovol.
Rankine	Isentropic	Isobaric	Isentropic	Isobaric

is the idealised steam cycle and therefore there are phase changes (vaporisation and condensation) of the fluid during the cycle.

thermodynamics The science of heat, work, temperature, etc., applied especially to 'heat engines' and the behaviour of gases. Thermodynamics is based on three fundamental laws: the first is equivalent to the law of **conservation of energy**; the second is to do with reversibility and the time-direction of physical processes, and leads to the definition of **entropy**; the third law concerns the absolute zero of temperature and its unattainability. To these three laws there is often prefixed a **zeroth law** basic to the definition of temperature.

Thermodynamics finds its main practical applications in the analysis of heat engines such as gas turbines, steam turbines, internal combustion engines, heat pumps and refrigerators. See also **thermodynamic cycles**.

thermoelectricity This term covers a set of three different but related phenomena known as the Seebeck effect, the Peltier effect and the Thomson (or Kelvin) effect.

The Seebeck effect is illustrated by Figure 45. An electrical cir-

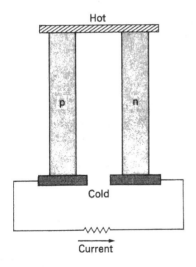

Figure 45 The Seebeck effect. p-type and n-type semiconductors are connected at a hot junction, other parts of the circuit being kept cool: the heat energy is partly converted into an electric current.

133

cuit has a high-temperature section linked to the rest of the circuit by two different pieces of material which can be p-type and n-type semiconductors. The heat generates a voltage which can be used to drive a current as shown; heat energy is thus converted directly into electric power. The conversion efficiency is low (5–10 per cent) but the method has been used in isotopic power generators driven by the decay heat of radioactive materials. The Seebeck effect is also used in thermocouples to measure temperature.

The Peltier effect is like the Seebeck effect in reverse. Instead of a temperature difference generating a voltage, an imposed voltage will cause heat to be transferred, one junction being heated and the other cooled. This principle can be applied to a **heat pump**, but the efficiency is low and there have been few applications.

The third effect, the Thomson effect, is a voltage gradient which will appear along a conducting wire when a temperature gradient is set up along it. This has no immediate application to energy technology.

theta pinch   A device to compress hot fusion fuel plasma. An enormous, mega-ampere-sized, electric current is produced from the discharge of a capacitor bank and passed around the outside of a plasma container shaped like a piece of pipe or tube. The resultant magnetic field squeezes the plasma into the central axis of the pipe, compressing it and heating it. In this way temperatures of 50,000,000 K have been achieved for short times.

Thomson effect   See **thermoelectricity**.

thorium   The element of atomic number $Z = 90$ (symbol Th). Thorium is one of the **actinide** metals, like uranium, but is more abundant than uranium in high-grade ores. It is found in the form of a single isotope, ^{232}Th, which is very slightly radioactive with a half-life of 14 thousand million years (see **geothermal energy**).

Thorium is 'fertile' in that it can be converted into a fissile material (^{233}U) through neutron absorption in a **breeder** reactor. In this way thorium could in principle contribute enormously to energy supplies in the future. Moreover, fuel cycles using thorium may turn out to be cleaner and less hazardous than those based on the alternative 'plutonium cycle'. See also **nuclear reactors**.

Three Mile Island   An island on the Susquehanna River near Harrisburg, Pennsylvania, and the site of a nuclear power plant where a pressurised water reactor suffered a severe overheating accident with partial melting of its core.

tidal energy The rise and fall of the ocean tides represents a renewable energy source which in principle could supply perhaps 1 EJ of energy per year as electricity throughout the world. In practice, however, its exploitation will be restricted to a few sites where there are large tidal ranges, such as the Bay of Fundy (Canada), Cook Inlet (Alaska), the Severn estuary (UK), and the Western Australian coast. There are already tidal energy installations in the USSR (near Murmansk) and France (the Rance estuary), the latter providing an electricity output of up to 250 MW.

Besides being available in practice at only a few sites, tidal energy has the economic disadvantage of requiring large capital expenditure and a long lead time before power is actually produced. It is therefore unlikely to make a substantial contribution to any country's energy supplies in the foreseeable future.

One of the schemes being actively investigated is that for the Severn estuary in the UK, shown on Figure 46. This would be equivalent to several gigawatt-sized power stations and could supply perhaps 6 per cent of UK electricity demand. The system illustrated (which is one of several options) consists of a 'high basin' filled at high tide, and a 'low basin' which is emptied at low tide. Electricity can be generated by letting water flow through the turbines between

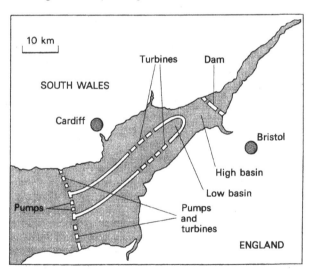

Figure 46 A tidal power scheme proposed for the Severn estuary. (After J. D. Denton *et al., The Potential of Natural Energy Sources,* CEGB, 1975, Fig. 10.)

135

these basins at any time, not just when the tide is at a particular height. A system like this therefore serves to store energy as well as to generate it and can provide load-following rather than baseload electricity. Furthermore, by including a set of pumps to transfer water up into the high basin, power produced elsewhere (e.g. in nuclear stations) can be stored with little loss.

tokamak (Russian for 'doughnut') The name given to a class of torus-shaped devices for the magnetic confinement of plasma in a nuclear **fusion reactor**.

ton A mass of 907.18 kg (see 'Units'). It is becoming more common to use not the ton but its metric counterpart, the tonne (1,000 kg).

transformer A device for altering the voltage of alternating-current electricity. A given amount of energy can be supplied either by a low current at high voltage, or by high current at low voltage, and for engineering and safety reasons has to be 'transformed' from a high voltage to successively lower voltages as it flows down the supply system to the electricity consumer.

transmission (1) In general, the movement of energy from one location to another, for example by electric power lines. Energy transmission involves losses which can amount to several per cent over a country the size of the UK, while over countries such as the USA or USSR the losses can be so great that it is scarcely practical to produce primary energy in regions remote from the centres of population and industry.
(2) In an automobile, the transmission is the set of machinery that transfers power from the engine to the driving wheels. It consists usually of the clutch, gearbox, propellor shaft and rear axle.

transport The movement of people and of goods accounts for a high proportion of energy consumption in all parts of the world, and it always has. This proportion is around 20 per cent in the developed world. In the case of personal transportation, Table 17 shows the energy expenditure needed to transport one person a distance of 1 kilometre. As one might expect, long-distance travel is more efficient than short-distance, and the figures are very sensitive to the numbers of seats filled in cars, buses, trains and aircraft. Transport energy accounting is further complicated by the energy-intensive construction required, e.g. for a railway system, and by the not insignificant denial of land to agriculture by road and rail networks.

136

Table 17 *Energy use of transport systems**

Transport system	Energy, MJ/passenger/km
Bus (inter-city)	0.4
Train (inter-city)	1.0
Bus (urban)	1.0
Train (urban)	1.4
Car (inter-city)**	1.6
Car (urban)***	3.1
Aircraft (scheduled)	3.9

*The above figures are an approximate guide to the running energy costs of transport systems, without regard to capital or land-use costs.
**Assumes on average 2 passengers.
***Assumes on average 1.5 passengers.

In the short term, plans for transport energy conservation are based on the more effective use of vehicles similar to those in use today: improved car engines developed in response to higher gasoline prices, the encouragement of rail use, and better air transport management. Such developments often depend, in ways not immediately obvious, on advances in microelectronics and communications technology.

In the longer term, the widening use of new energy sources and new propulsion systems can be expected. Data on some are given in Table 18: this shows the efficiency with which transport fuels can be produced and delivered from primary fuels, and also the usage efficiencies (storage medium, motor and transmission) for a combustion engine, an electric motor based on storage cells and one based on fuel cells. One can see, for example, that if coal is converted into a liquid hydrocarbon fuel and burnt in combustion heat engines, the overall efficiency is something like $0.6 \times 0.2 = 0.12$, whereas if electricity is generated from the coal and used in storage cells for electric traction engines, the efficiency is $0.3 \times 0.5 = 0.15$. However, it must be stressed that transport power is an active research field in which rapid advances are constantly being made. For example, there are now numerous types of **storage cell** under development with efficiencies being pushed higher all the time.

One of the reasons for current interest in electric traction is the effective use that can be made of electricity, be it primary electricity (from nuclear stations or hydro schemes) or coal-generated electricity. In this way there is hope that oil can be displaced, at least in part, in road and rail transport.

Table 18 *Efficiencies for fuel conversion and for fuel use in transport**

	Delivered fuel		
	Electricity	Methane	Liquid fuel
Primary fuel:			
Coal	0.3	0.65	0.6
Natural gas	0.3	0.95	—
Crude oil	0.3	—	0.9
Prim. electricity	0.9	—	—
Transport use efficiency:			
Heat engine	—	0.2	0.2
Elec. storage cell	0.5	—	—
Fuel cell	—	0.35	0.35

*These figures are approximate values of the current energy efficiencies for fuel conversion (above) and the subsequent use of the fuel in transport.

Another possibility in the long term is that changing patterns of urbanisation and habitation might reduce the need for transport, with a decentralisation of labour-intensive industries and the exploitation of telecommunications to the full.

In the future, it is unlikely that transport will be dominated by a single fuel to the same degree that it is today. As well as oil products, there will be roles for methane, hydrogen, coal-derived liquid fuel, alcohol and electricity.

transuranic elements   The elements with atomic number greater than that of uranium, i.e. with Z greater than 92. They are heavy elements which are unstable and do not occur in nature; the most notable is **plutonium**. The transuranic elements comprise the top end of the **actinide** series followed by the elements 104 *et seq*.

Element 104 is known as kurchatovium (Ku) or rutherfordium (Rf), and element 105 is called hahnium (Ha) or nielsbohrium (Ns), alternative names having arisen because of dispute between American and Russian groups over priority of discovery.

Elements 106 and, probably, 107 have also been identified but not yet named; however, it is common to refer to heavy unnamed elements by the prefix 'eka' in front of the element standing above in the periodic table. For example, element 107 is ekarhenium and element 112 would be ekamercury.

---

triple point   Most substances can exist in gaseous, liquid and solid forms; the triple point is the combination of temperature and pressure at which all three forms may coexist.

tritium   The isotope of hydrogen with a nucleus consisting of one proton and two neutrons. Its symbol is T, or alternatively ^{3}H. Tritium is radioactive, beta-decaying with a half-life of 12.3 years.

Tritium is likely to be useful as a nuclear **fusion** fuel, and although it occurs hardly at all in nature it can be 'bred' out of the abundant metal lithium.

Trombe wall   An architectural idea on which a passive solar heating system can be based; see **domestic energy**. The Trombe wall is a massive concrete south-facing wall outside which is a layer of glazing. The wall absorbs and stores solar heat, and the glass prevents re-radiation or convection loss to the outside. The air in the space between the concrete and the glass is warmed and can be ducted in to heat the living space.

A Trombe wall has the advantage that in hot weather it can have a cooling effect, the solar heat being discharged at the top of the wall and drawing a current of air through the building from the cooler north side.

Trouton's rule   The empirical rule that for most liquids

$$L_b \sim T_b \cdot 10R$$

L_b being the latent heat of boiling, T_b the boiling temperature, and R the universal 'gas constant' equal to 8.32 joules per degree per mole. Trouton's rule would tell us, for example, that a refrigerant boiling at 27 C (300 K) will take up a latent heat of 24.7 kJ mol^{-1} (actual value for CC1$_3$F is 25.0 kJ mol^{-1}), while water boiling at 100 C (373 K) will take up 31 kJ mol^{-1} (actual value 40.6).

turbine   Any device that transforms a flow of liquid or gas into a rotary mechanical movement by means of a fan-like or propellor-like array of blades.

Steam turbines are widely used to drive electrical generators from steam raised in fossil-fuel-burning or nuclear power plants. The efficiency of a steam turbine is severely restricted by thermodynamical laws, but up to 50 per cent has been achieved.

Gas turbines, driven by combustion gases from gas or liquid fuels, are often used for electricity generation in small or medium-sized plants; they can also be used to propel vehicles of all kinds. In aircraft, turbojet and turboprop engines are forms of gas turbine.

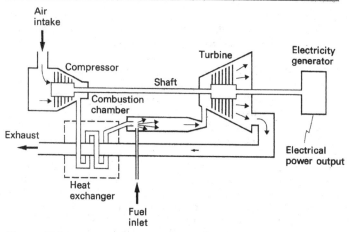

Figure 47 Schematic diagram of a gas turbine plant.

Figure 47 shows the main principles of the gas turbine: hot gas from fuel combustion blasts through the turbine blades and rotates the shaft, and then the exhaust can be passed through a heat exchanger to preheat fresh air which is being blown into the combustion chamber. In the arrangement illustrated the shaft drives not only an electricity generator but also a compressor for the input fresh air, thereby making a substantial improvement to the overall efficiency.

Wind turbines of many different types have been devised to extract power from natural currents of air. For examples, see **wind energy**, **Savonius rotor**.

Water power has been harnessed with turbines of various types: the Pelton turbine consists of paddles or buckets around the edge of a large wheel, with water directed tangentially against them; the traditional 'waterwheel' is of this type. Another type is the Kaplan turbine, which is similar in appearance to a ship's propellor and is fixed in a tube-like channel through which the water is ducted. The Francis turbine, which is very commonly used, works in a slightly more complex way and is illustrated in Figure 48. The water is directed round in a spiral path, gives up its momentum to the turbine blades, and is discharged through the centre.

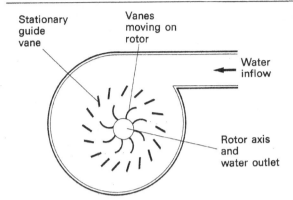

Figure 48 The Francis turbine. Water is directed on an inward spiral path to power a rotor; it then flows away down through a central sink (the diagram is a plan view).

UCS Union of Concerned Scientists.

UKAEA United Kingdom Atomic Energy Authority.

ultra-violet (UV) Electromagnetic radiation with frequency lying above that of the blue end of the visible light spectrum. The ultra-violet wavelength range is taken to be 0.005 to 0.4 microns.

UV radiation consists of more energetic quanta than ordinary light and can be harmful to life. The UV from the sun, however, is screened off from the surface of the earth by substances (notably ozone) in the upper atmosphere.

Union of Concerned Scientists A group of scientists formed in 1969 in the Boston area, USA, to examine the problems to public health and safety of the nuclear industry. The UCS has since established itself as an influential and objective body although taking a broadly antinuclear stance.

141

United Kingdom Atomic Energy Authority (UKAEA) The British government body responsible for nuclear reactor operation and research.

uranium The element of atomic number $Z = 92$ (symbol U). Uranium is the heaviest element which occurs naturally on the earth and is one of the **actinide** metals. It is of importance because one of its isotopes, ^{235}U, can be made to undergo nuclear fission with the release of an amount of energy which is enormous compared with the chemical energy released by combustible fuels such as coal.

The fissile isotope, ^{235}U, amounts to only 0.7% of natural uranium; the other 99.3% is ^{238}U, a non-fissile and not immediately useful isotope. This disproportion in quantities has its origin in the fact that ^{235}U is radioactive, with a half-life of 710 million years, and so has become greatly diminished since the earth was formed about 4,600 million years ago. The other isotope, ^{238}U, is also radioactive but to a much lesser extent, the half-life being 4,500 million years.

^{235}U is the most common fuel for energy-producing nuclear reactors, but it is extremely difficult to separate it from ^{238}U. Most reactors are therefore designed to take 'enriched' uranium with the ^{235}U fraction increased to a few per cent. This means that a good deal of non-fissile ^{238}U is put through reactors without contributing to the energy output, but there are sound engineering and economic reasons for it. Moreover, by putting ^{238}U through reactors there is a further bonus in that it 'breeds' plutonium, which is a fissile material from which energy can be got in suitably-designed reactors.

Besides ^{235}U and ^{238}U there is a third uranium isotope of importance, namely ^{233}U. This is not found in nature (its half-life is 160,000 years) but it can be bred from thorium. ^{233}U is a fissile substance which provides a way of deriving energy from the large reserves of thorium which exist.

Uranium is not a rare metal, and has been found throughout the world. Perhaps three million tons of it can be extracted at moderate price. Uranium reserves, like those of other mineral resources, are difficult to quantify with precision because of the patchy nature of exploration worldwide and because for political and commercial reasons information is not always made public. Furthermore, since large amounts of energy can be got from small amounts of uranium fuel, the price is very elastic, and it may become economic to use very low grade deposits from which uranium is expensive but enormously abundant. At the extreme, uranium could be got from seawater which contains about 1.2 parts per billion of the metal.

See also **enrichment, nuclear reactors, breeder, geothermal energy.**

142

U-value   A measure of how quickly heat will pass through a wall, roof or other insulating surface. It is expressed in terms of watts per square metre per degree (C or K) of temperature difference across the surface. A typical U-value for a modern house might be $3\ \text{W m}^{-2}\ \text{K}^{-1}$, averaging over walls, windows and roof: with a total surface area of, say, $100\ \text{m}^2$, this gives a heat loss of 3 kW if the inside is 10 degrees warmer than the outside.

For a surface consisting of a thickness t of a single material, the U-value is given by

$$U = k/t$$

where k is the thermal **conductivity** of the material. For a compound wall with different thicknesses of different materials, one adds the reciprocals of the U-values, i.e.

$$U^{-1}_{\text{compound}} = U^{-1}_a + U^{-1}_b + U^{-1}_c + \ldots$$

where U_a, U_b, etc., are the U-values of the different layers.

vapour compression cycle   This is the principle of operation of the majority of **heat pumps**, and in particular the bulk of domestic refrigerators. A fluid passes around the cycle, partly in liquid and partly in vapour form, as shown in Figure 49. Heat is taken in by the fluid at a point in the cycle where both temperature and pres-

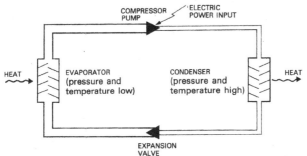

Figure 49 Principle of the vapour compression cycle.

143

sure are low; this heat does not raise the temperature of the fluid but it causes some to evaporate, i.e. it becomes 'latent' heat. The vapour is then drawn through a compressor pump which increases the pressure and, at the same time, the temperature of the vapour. It can then be passed through a condenser, heat being given up to the (cooler) surroundings while vapour turns back to liquid. To complete the cycle, an expansion valve or nozzle lets fluid pass back to the low-pressure, cold side of the cycle.

The net effect is to transfer heat from a cool region, such as the inside of a refrigerator, to a warmer one; it is at the expense of an input of power to the compressor pump. Used as a heat pump, the vapour compression cycle can transfer something like three times as much energy in the form of heat as it consumes as electricity. See also **refrigerants, thermodynamic cycles, absorption cycle**.

vapour cycle A general term for any system in which a vapour or gas is compressed and/or expanded in a controlled way so that there is an interchange between heat energy and mechanical energy. Refrigerators commonly operate through vapour cycles; another example is the turbine motor which converts the energy of high-temperature gas into mechanical work.

vitrification A process involving high-temperature heat treatment under pressure by which substances may be converted into a solid glass-like form. The vitrification of radioactive waste material from the nuclear energy industry can improve safety because it becomes inert and insoluble (the waste, I mean, not the industry) and can be stored for long periods without hazard.

volt (V) The standard unit for measuring electric potential. When a source of electrical power drives a current, the energy produced (its rate measured in watts) is equal to the current (in amps) multiplied by the potential of the source (in volts).

Wankel engine A kind of internal combustion engine used in some types of automobile instead of the conventional reciprocating piston engine. The Wankel engine has the theoretical advantage that it produces power directly in the form of rotary motion through a carefully shaped rotary 'piston' that spins in the combustion chamber; there is no need for a crankshaft.

waste Any unusable by-product of a biological, commercial or industrial process. Heavy waste production is often associated with inefficient energy use, and an analysis of waste is a good starting point for the planning of a conservation programme. Agricultural waste can often be utilised as a **biological energy** source, waste heat from power stations can be recovered through CHP systems; even domestic refuse can be burned to give useful energy. **Nuclear waste** is an important constraint on the nuclear energy industry, and may be regarded as a symptom of fundamental inefficiency in the way uranium is used.

waterwheel An early device for converting the energy of a running stream into useful rotary power. Waterwheels have been used for pumping, milling and operating forges. In the present day they are occasionally used for electricity generation, but hydraulic turbines of more modern design are preferred.

watt (W) The conventional unit to measure a rate of flow of energy. One watt amounts to 1 joule per second. See also **energy**, 'Units'.

wave energy The energy in the waves arises from wind across the surfaces of the ocean and so is constantly renewed from, ultimately, the sun. At any moment there is probably something like an exajoule of energy in the waves that is being dissipated and renewed at several terawatts.

To extract useful energy from the waves a number of devices, some very ingenious, have been proposed. Unfortunately, the working environment poses a number of obvious engineering difficulties and there is no immediate prospect of a commercial device becoming available.

wellhead cost The cost of bringing oil or gas to the surface, before the costs of transport, refining, taxes and so on have been added.

Weston cell A type of electric storage cell, used not so much to provide energy as to be a standard of voltage.

wind energy The energy of motion within the earth's atmosphere, amounting to the order of 100 EJ (10^{20} J), which is constantly maintained by the movement of the earth and by solar energy.

Wind energy has traditionally been exploited by windmills or wind pumps, and during this century by electrical wind-energy machines ('aerogenerators'). Aerogenerator designs may be divided into two categories, namely horizontal-axis machines like traditional windmills, and vertical-axis machines of more novel appearance.

As an example, the Darrieus type of vertical-axis aerogenerator is illustrated in Figure 50. The curving vanes have a subtly designed

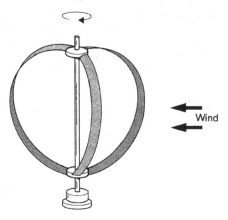

Figure 50 The Darrieus vertical-axis aerogenerator.

cross-sectional shape, like aircraft wings, so that the movement of the air will make them rotate around the central pillar. Unlike that of horizontal-axis machines, this sort of design avoids the need for the aerogenerator to be pointed towards the wind. See also **Savonius rotor.**

Aerogenerators have been built and operated with power outputs of well over 1 MW, and proposals have been made for them to be used on a very wide scale in the future. A difficulty is that such machines would be at least 50 or 100 metres in height, and aesthetically unpleasing if erected on the high, open countryside where they would be most effective. Another problem is that in most countries the ideal sites tend to be thinly-populated mountainous or coastal areas, remote from the centres of population and industry which need the energy; the electricity distribution system therefore imposes constraints on the viability of large-scale electricity production from the wind.

Small domestic aerogenerators have been successfully marketed which give a few kW of electricity under favourable wind conditions and are useful to consumers who value an independent electricity supply with negligible running cost. Their use could become widespread where electricity prices are high relative to manufacturing and maintenance costs.

window   One of the most important energy-transmission devices in a building. It is now realised that window design is essential to achieve good energy efficiency, the following being the major considerations: (a) to minimise heat loss by conduction through the window, by using thick glass and/or double glazing, and by using wind screens to reduce air flow over the outer surface, (b) to minimise the loss of warm air through cracks around badly-fitting windows, (c) to maximise the 'solar gain' of radiant energy, and also the benefit of light from the sun to save electric illumination, (d) to minimise radiant heat loss through windows, e.g. by the use of special optical coatings on the glass, (e) in hot weather, not to give excessive heat from the sun which would need to be countered by energy-consuming air conditioners.

Windscale   Site in Cumbria, UK, where the first British reactors for plutonium production were set up shortly after the Second World War, along with facilities for the reprocessing of nuclear fuel. There is now also a successful AGR at Windscale. There has been controversy over a decision to build at Windscale a commercial reprocessing plant for the final treatment of used uranium oxide fuel from thermal nuclear reactors. See also **reprocessing**.

wood   Still a major source of energy as a fuel, accounting for perhaps 10 per cent of world energy consumption. Most wood fuel is used in the less developed southern countries, but roughly as much again is used in the developed world in construction, paper-making, etc.
 Wood, which has a calorific value of around 16 MJ/kg, consists largely of the carbohydrate cellulose. See also **fuels, biological energy**.

work   Mechanical energy, measured in joules.

xenon A gaseous element, with atomic number $Z = 54$ and symbol Xe, occurring in a wide variety of isotopes with mass number A ranging from 124 to 137. It is produced abundantly as a fission product by nuclear reactors. Some isotopes are radioactive, and in particular ^{133}Xe persists for some days and can therefore constitute a safety hazard. Another isotope, ^{135}Xe, has a high probability in a reactor of absorbing neutrons and so degrading the efficiency of the reactor.

X-ray A burst of electromagnetic radiation with wavelength in the range 10^{-12} to 10^{-9} m, i.e. much shorter and thereby more energetic than visible light. X-rays may be emitted in certain nuclear decay processes, and also may be given off by beta-rays as they pass through matter.

yellowcake Processed uranium ore, in the form of uranium oxides or ammonium or sodium diuranate. Quantities and prices are usually quoted in terms of the equivalent amount of the oxide U_3O_8.

zeroth law The zeroth law of thermodynamics, so numbered because it is fundamental to the first, second and third laws (for which see **thermodynamics**), but was only later recognised as being a non-

148

trivial law in its own right. The zeroth law states that if two systems are separately in thermal equilibrium with a third, then they must also be in thermal equilibrium with each other. 'In thermal equilibrium' means, in effect, 'at the same temperature', and this law thereby underlies the concept and definition of temperature.

ZETA (zero-energy thermonuclear apparatus) An early device built at Harwell, Oxon., to attempt the magnetic confinement of plasma for nuclear fusion.

zircaloy A metallic alloy used for cladding the fissile fuel in some nuclear reactors. It is chosen because of its properties of resistance to heat and corrosion and of good neutron economy, and it consists mostly of the element zirconium.

International energy statistics

For any country, the pattern of energy production and consumption is crucial in determining standards of living, the level of agricultural and industrial activity, the rate of development, and so forth. The information in this section (Table 19) amounts to an 'energy profile' for every country whose population exceeds one million; since it is in a condensed form some explanation of the data is necessary, and further below some examples are taken of particular countries. The table contains:

(a) The annual energy consumption (C) per capita, measured in gigajoules. For conversion to other units see Tables B and C.

(b) The population in millions. The restriction to countries with more than one million inhabitants removes about 1.5 per cent of the world's population.

(c) The national ratio of energy production to energy consumption (P/C). Production includes crude fossil fuels, wood and primary electricity (i.e. hydro and nuclear electricity), whereas consumption includes gas, coal, refined liquid fuels (including what is used for central electricity production), wood and that proportion of electricity attributable to primary sources.

The production to consumption ratio for the world as a whole, given at the end of the table, is 1.06, the excess over unity being due to oil. Crude oil and refined oil products are generally accounted in different ways, and the refining process itself takes up some energy.

(d) The percentage breakdown of energy consumption between primary electricity (PE), fossil fuels (FF) and wood (Wd). It must be borne in mind that data for wood consumption are very uncertain, since wood by its very nature is gathered and used in an uncontrolled way. In fact the less developed a country is, the more it is likely to depend on wood fuel and the more difficult it is to quantify the consumption of wood with any precision. The Table gives 7 per cent as the world average of wood fuel as a proportion of total consumption, but other less conservative estimates have been made which range up into double figures: it may therefore be that half as much again should be added to the figures for wood consumption.

(e) Of the fossil fuels consumed, the final column gives the percentages of coal (i.e. all solid fossil fuels), oil and gas.

These statistics are largely derived from United Nations figures and they apply to the year 1978. Care should be taken in using them, since data of this kind are always unreliable in so far as precise statistics are not collected or are not released by many countries, and some educated guesswork has had to be used. In many cases the population is less certain than the Table might suggest.

These reservations apart, Table 19 contains the essential information on energy for all but the smallest of the world's nations. To take a simple example first, Hong Kong had a consumption of 48.6 GJ per capita in 1978, and while this is well below the level of the Western developed world it is very substantial compared with other parts of South-East Asia or China itself. Since the population was 4.6 million, the total consumption was 224 PJ. Since the P/C ratio is given as zero, all this energy was imported, and it can be seen that it took the form entirely of one fossil fuel, namely oil. From Table C we see that one tonne of oil is roughly the equivalent of 44.8 GJ, and so Hong Kong must have imported some 5 million tonnes of oil in the year. As a glance through the figures will show, Hong Kong is one of a small but important group of nations which are not unprosperous but which produce little or no energy in any form, being entirely dependent on imported oil. This group includes nations such as Cuba, Israel, Jamaica, Jordan and Singapore.

Iraq is a good example of a large oil-producing country. It is not yet well developed and so consumes little more than 18.6 GJ per capita per annum, i.e. a total of about 230 PJ per annum, about the same as Hong Kong. However, Iraq has no need of energy imports, as it produces two dozen times the amount it consumes. Iraq's consumption is mostly of oil, but a good deal of gas, found with the oil, is also used up. Referring again to Table C, it can be expressed as nearly four million tonnes of oil and two thousand million cubic metres of gas.

A very different kind of energy profile is exemplified by Mali. Mali might at first glance seem close to self-sufficiency in energy, producing 90 per cent of its consumption; but closer inspection reveals that the 90 per cent is accounted for by wood fuel. The remaining 10 per cent, which must be imported, takes the form of oil, and is equivalent to over 100 thousand tonnes per annum. With a consumption per capita of only 8.1 GJ per annum, Mali is close to the bottom of the developmental ladder.

As a final example we may consider Finland, which partly for climatic reasons consumes a high 170 GJ per capita annually. About 7 per cent is primary electricity, in this case hydroelectric rather than nuclear. 10 per cent or so is provided by wood. These renewable sources account for almost all of Finland's energy production (18 per cent of the consumption) and it can therefore be taken that the amounts of coal, oil and gas listed are mostly imported.

151

The last line of Table 19 gives the world situation: over four billion people, with an energy consumption per head averaging out at about half that in, say, France, and of which 90 per cent is provided by fossil fuels. In spite of the theoretical potential of nuclear energy and of hydroelectricity, these together account for only 3 per cent or so at the present time. The 7 per cent quoted for wood-burning may be a small percentage but it is vital in numerous emergent nations; for ecological reasons one would not wish wood to be used to any greater extent. Of the fossil fuels, oil is at the moment predominant but will run into short supply within a few decades, and there is a widely-held belief that coal will re-emerge as man's major primary energy source.

Table 19 *International energy statistics*

Country	C per capita (GJ)	Pop.	P/C	C (%) PE/FF/Wd	FF C (%) coal/oil/gas
Afghanistan	6.7	17.9	1.69	2/19/79	22/74/4
Albania	38.7	2.7	1.68	7/69/24	22/68/10
Algeria	21.5	18.5	7.45	0/95/5	2/50/48
Angola	20.9	6.8	3.25	2/25/73	0/92/8
Argentina	56.9	26.4	0.92	2/94/4	3/71/26
Australia	196.	14.2	1.35	2/97/1	48/42/10
Austria	121.	7.5	0.35	9/89/2	20/56/24
Bangladesh	3.1	84.6	0.76	1/39/60	11/51/38
Belgium	178.	9.8	0.14	2/98/0	24/53/23
Benin	12.1	3.4	0.85	1/14/85	0/100/0
Bolivia	11.8	6.1	2.08	5/87/8	0/92/8
Brazil	38.9	115.	0.60	8/52/40	11/87/2
Bulgaria	149.	8.8	0.33	3/96/1	45/45/10
Burma	11.6	32.2	1.03	1/15/84	11/77/12
Burundi	3.7	4.1	0.95	1/6/93	16/84/0
Cameroun	18.5	6.8	0.85	4/15/81	0/100/0
Canada	294.	23.5	1.12	12/87/1	13/56/31
Cent. Africa	16.1	1.9	0.94	1/5/94	0/100/0
Chad	12.8	4.3	0.95	0/5/95	0/100/0
Chile	33.9	10.9	0.60	6/80/14	16/75/9
China	26.9	916.	1.02	1/90/9	81/18/1
Colombia	32.9	25.9	1.02	4/58/38	24/58/18
Congo	30.4	1.2	2.82	1/16/83	0/93/7
Costa Rica	33.2	2.1	0.58	8/42/50	0/100/0
Cuba	36.5	10.1	0.07	0/94/6	1/99/0
Czechoslov.	223.	15.1	0.73	1/98/1	71/22/7
Denmark	159.	5.1	0.02	0/100/0	18/82/0
Dom'can Rp.	18.8	5.1	0.27	0/73/27	0/100/0
Ecuador	18.7	7.8	3.14	2/77/21	0/98/2
Egypt	13.6	39.6	1.86	6/94/0	7/85/8

Country	C per capita (GJ)	Pop.	P/C	C (%) PE/FF/Wd	FF C (%) coal/oil/gas
El Salvador	17.9	4.5	0.61	4/39/57	0/100/0
Ethiopia	12.8	29.7	0.96	0/4/96	0/100/0
Finland	170.	4.8	0.18	7/83/10	21/74/5
France	129.	53.3	0.20	5/94/1	21/66/13
German D.R.	209.	16.8	0.70	1/99/0	73/20/7
German F.R.	177.	61.3	0.45	2/98/0	32/50/17
Ghana	18.7	10.8	0.83	7/17/76	1/99/0
Greece	59.6	9.4	0.29	1/94/5	27/73/0
Guatemala	19.3	6.6	0.63	1/38/61	0/100/0
Guinea	11.6	4.8	0.77	1/23/76	0/100/0
Haiti	12.6	4.8	0.88	1/12/87	0/100/0
Honduras	21.9	3.3	0.65	2/35/63	0/100/0
Hong Kong	48.6	4.6	0	0/100/0	0/100/0
Hungary	104.	10.7	0.59	2/95/3	37/39/25
India	8.2	638.	0.90	3/61/36	69/30/2
Indonesia	20.1	147.	1.99	0/41/59	1/85/14
Iran*	53.8	35.2	6.63	1/97/2	2/54/44
Iraq	18.6	12.3	24.5	0/100/0	0/72/28
Ireland	96.6	3.2	0.24	1/99/0	30/70/0
Israel	69.1	3.7	0.01	0/100/0	0/99/1
Italy	95.4	56.7	0.14	4/95/1	7/73/20
Ivory Coast	25.3	5.3	0.60	1/39/60	0/100/0
Jamaica	53.6	2.1	0	0/100/0	0/100/0
Japan	112.	115.	0.08	3/97/0	18/77/5
Jordan	15.8	3.0	0	0/100/0	0/100/0
Kampuchea	7.3	8.9	0.98	0/1/99	0/100/0
Kenya	18.7	14.9	0.79	1/21/78	3/97/0
Korean D.P.R.	83.3	17.1	0.96	4/91/5	96/4/0
Korean Rp.	42.6	37.0	0.40	1/93/6	38/62/0
Kuwait	198.	1.2	20.1	0/100/0	0/32/68
Laos	15.5	3.6	0.91	1/10/89	0/100/0
Lebanon	27.9	3.3	0.04	3/96/1	0/100/0
Liberia	26.6	1.8	0.59	2/41/57	0/100/0
Libya	58.7	2.5	29.5	0/94/6	0/100/0
Madagascar	10.9	8.8	0.80	1/20/79	4/96/0
Malawi	9.9	5.4	0.87	2/13/85	28/72/0
Malaysia	27.7	13.2	1.41	1/75/24	0/89/10
Mali	8.1	6.2	0.90	0/10/90	0/100/0
Mauritania	11.7	1.4	0.50	0/50/50	2/98/0
Mexico	42.4	66.9	1.27	3/93/4	9/70/21
Mongolia	49.4	1.6	0.74	0/73/27	65/35/0
Morocco	10.7	19.2	0.37	2/76/22	13/85/2
Mozambique	17.2	9.9	0.87	1/25/74	50/50/0

*Pre-revolution data.

153

International energy statistics

Country	C per capita (GJ)	Pop.	P/C	C (%) PE/FF/Wd	FF C (%) coal/oil/gas
Netherlands	157.	13.9	1.32	1/99/0	6/39/56
Nepal	10.2	13.4	0.97	0/3/97	7/93/0
New Zealand	112.	3.1	0.58	17/82/1	17/62/21
Nicaragua	41.4	2.4	0.35	1/66/33	0/100/0
Niger	9.4	4.5	0.87	0/13/87	0/100/0
Nigeria	17.3	68.6	4.07	1/17/82	4/86/10
Norway	165.	4.1	2.27	40/59/1	8/89/2
Pakistan	6.8	76.8	0.74	4/70/26	7/42/51
Panama	40.4	1.8	0.30	1/71/28	0/100/0
Pap. N. Guin.	34.0	3.0	0.76	1/24/75	3/97/0
Paraguay	23.9	2.9	0.78	2/23/75	0/100/0
Peru	24.6	16.8	1.07	6/71/23	2/91/7
Phillipines	18.0	46.4	0.48	2/53/45	2/98/0
Poland	165.	35.0	1.09	0/100/0	83/11/6
Portugal	31.1	9.8	0.16	11/86/3	7/93/0
Puerto Rico	137.	3.0	0	0/100/0	0/100/0
Romania	122.	21.7	0.92	1/96/3	22/26/52
Rwanda	12.7	4.8	0.98	1/2/97	0/98/2
Saudi Arabia	38.3	9.8	48.1	0/100/0	0/93/7
Senegal	14.5	4.8	0.64	0/36/64	0/100/0
Sierra Leone	14.6	3.2	0.81	0/19/81	0/100/0
Singapore	72.1	2.3	0	0/100/0	0/100/0
Somalia	18.0	3.4	0.84	0/16/84	0/100/0
Spain	71.7	36.7	0.28	7/91/2	24/73/3
Sri Lanka	7.5	14.9	0.61	4/39/57	0/100/0
Sudan	29.4	16.9	0.83	0/17/83	0/100/0
Sweden	180.	8.3	0.21	17/80/3	5/95/0
Switzerland	110.	6.3	0.23	18/80/2	2/93/5
Syria	28.6	8.1	1.99	3/97/0	0/91/9
Tanzania	36.7	16.6	0.95	0/5/95	0/100/0
Thailand	15.1	45.1	0.40	2/62/36	1/99/0
Togo	9.1	2.4	0.68	2/30/68	0/100/0
Trinidad	146.	1.1	3.72	0/100/0	0/42/58
Tunisia	20.6	6.1	1.79	0/78/22	3/85/12
Turkey	33.1	43.2	0.54	2/68/30	23/77/0
Uganda	17.6	12.8	0.93	1/7/92	0/100/0
UK	153.	55.8	0.84	2/98/0	38/41/21
Upper Volta	10.0	6.5	0.92	0/8/92	0/100/0
Uruguay	35.7	2.9	0.20	6/80/14	1/99/0
USA	334.	220.	0.81	2/98/0	21/48/31
USSR	165.	263.	1.28	2/95/3	35/36/29
Venezuela	96.9	13.1	4.36	4/87/9	1/51/48
Viet Nam	8.7	49.3	1.00	1/41/58	85/15/0
Yemen	1.6	7.3	0	0/100/0	0/100/0
Yemen (Dem.)	15.5	1.8	0	0/100/0	0/100/0

Country	C per capita (GJ)	Pop.	P/C	C (%) PE/FF/Wd	FF C (%) coal/oil/gas
Yugoslavia	62.6	21.9	0.64	6/89/5	44/50/6
Zaire	8.5	27.7	1.05	6/18/76	20/80/0
Zambia	28.9	5.5	0.85	14/34/52	41/59/0
Zimbabwe	28.9	6.9	0.84	11/48/41	72/28/0
World	65.1	4220.	1.06	3/90/7	33/47/20

Bibliography

What follows is not intended to be a complete and comprehensive bibliography of energy: if it were, it would fill this book many times over. Instead, a selective list is given of those books which have been found especially useful in the writing of this dictionary and in the teaching of the author's courses at Southampton University. Journal articles, which in a fast-moving field like this are at least as important as books, are not listed here; nor has any attempt been made to list the unpublished material distributed by private institutions. Such sources are essential for any serious study of a topic in the energy field, and the reader seeking guidance should consult his local university.

Adkins, C., *Equilibrium Thermodynamics*, McGraw-Hill, London, 1968.

Armstead, H., *Geothermal Energy*, Spon, London, 1978.

Camatini, E. and Kester, T., *Heat Pumps and Their Contribution to Energy Conservation*, Noordhoff International, Leyden, 1976.

Cole, G., *The Structure of Planets*, Wykeham, London, 1978.

Congress of the United States, *Nuclear Proliferation and Safeguards*, Praeger, New York, 1977.

Crabbe, D. and McBride, R., *The World Energy Book*, Kogan Page, London, 1978.

Foley, G., *The Energy Question*, Penguin, London, 1976.

Foster, A. and Wright, R., *Basic Nuclear Engineering*, Allyn & Bacon, Boston, 1973.

Fowler, J., *Energy and the Environment*, McGraw-Hill, New York, 1975.

Garrels, R. et al., *Chemical Cycles and the Global Environment*, William Kaufmann, Los Altos, Calif., 1975.

Graves, H., *Nuclear Fuel Management*, Wiley, New York, 1979.

Lamarsh, J., *Introduction to Nuclear Engineering*, Addison-Wesley, Reading, Mass., 1975.

Landsberg, P., *Thermodynamics and Statistical Mechanics*, Oxford University Press, 1978.

Leach, G., *A Low Energy Strategy for the United Kingdom*, Science Reviews, London, 1979.

Liverhant, S., *Nuclear Reactor Physics*, Wiley, New York, 1960.

Lovins, A., *Soft Energy Paths*, Penguin, London, 1977.

de Montbrial, T., *Energy: the Countdown*, Pergamon, London, 1979.

Nader, R. and Abbots, J., *The Menace of Atomic Energy*, W.W. Norton, New York, 1977.

Patterson, W., *Nuclear Power*, Penguin, London, 1976.

Penner, S.S. and Icerman, L., *Energy*, Addison-Wesley, Reading, Mass., 1975.

Reay, D., *Industrial Energy Conservation*, Pergamon, London, 1979.

Rochlin, G. (ed.), *Scientific Technology and Social Change*, W.H. Freeman, San Francisco, 1974.

Sayigh, A., *Solar Energy Engineering*, Academic Press, New York, 1977.

Shepard, M. *et al.*, *Introduction to Energy Technology*, Ann Arbor Science Publishers, 1976.

Sherrat, A., *Energy Conservation and Energy Management in Buildings*, Applied Science Publishers, London, 1976.

Simeons, C., *Coal: its Role in Tomorrow's Technology*, Pergamon, London, 1978.

Slesser, M., *Energy in the Economy*, Macmillan, London, 1978.

Slesser, M. and Lewis, C., *Biological Energy Resources*, Spon, London, 1979.

Starr, C., *Current Issues in Energy*, Pergamon, London, 1979.

Stobaugh, R. and Yergin, D. (eds), *Energy Future*, Random House, New York, 1979.

Teller, E., *Energy from Heaven and Earth*, W.H. Freeman, San Francisco, 1979.

United Nations, *World Energy Supplies 1973-1978*, United Nations, New York, 1979.

Ward, B., *Progress for a Small Planet*, Penguin, London, 1979.